The Secret Language of

DREAMS

The Secret Language of Dreams

A VISUAL KEY TO DREAMS AND THEIR MEANINGS

DAVID FONTANA

with paintings by Peter Malone

PIATKUS

This paperback edition published in 1997 by
Judy Piatkus (Publishers) Limited
5 Windmill Street
London W1P 1HF

First published in Great Britain in 1994 by
Pavilion Books Limited

A DBP book,
conceived, edited and designed by
Duncan Baird Publishers
Sixth Floor
Castle House
75–76 Wells Street
London W1P 3RE

Designers: *Paul Reid, Sue Bush*
Editor: *Richard Waterstone*
Commissioned Artwork: *Peter Malone*
Commissioned Photography and Photographic Illustrations:
Jules Selmes
Picture Research: *Jan Croot*
Props: *Eliza Solesbury*

A catalogue record for this book is available from the British Library

ISBN 0-7499-1757-1

Typeset in Perpetua
Colour reproduction by Colourscan, Singapore
Printed by Imago, Singapore

"Dreams are a conversation with oneself, a dialogue of symbols and images that takes place between the unconscious and conscious levels of the mind."

Contents

CONTENTS

Perspectives on the Dream World

We live in two worlds, the waking world with its laws of science, logic and social behaviour, and the elusive world of dreaming, still shrouded in mystery behind the veil of sleep. In the dream world, fantastic happenings, images and transformations are normal currency. Often such dream experiences are suffused with a depth of emotion or visionary insight that can surpass waking experience.

Historically, most of the world's cultures have believed that dreams come from an outside source, as visitations from the gods. The Egyptians believed that dreams carried messages from good and bad spirits, the Greeks built special shrines to serve as dream oracles. Even as late as the last century, people have interpreted the horrifying apparitions in nightmares as demons intent on seducing the innocent. Such obsolete interpretations are explored in the first half of "Perspectives on the Dream World".

Modern dream study begins only with Sigmund Freud (1856-1939), who located dreams in the unconscious, where our repressed instincts and desires dwell. The groundbreaking theories of Carl Jung (1875-1961) concerning archetypes and the collective unconscious were in many ways a direct response to Freud. Inevitably these two figures loom large in any serious book on dreaming.

The identification of REM (Rapid Eye Movement) sleep in 1953 brought technology to bear on dream research, in order to explore the physiology of dreaming and the relationship between dreams and sleep. The latter half of "Perspectives on the Dream World" analyzes this relationship, and concludes by demonstrating how dream precognition, once thought to be the domain of mystics and charlatans, has in recent years been studied and tested in dream laboratories.

Dreaming Through History

All through history we have sought to fathom the meanings of our dreams. Intrigued by their strange images, and their apparent cargo of symbolism, we have searched them energetically for insights into our present lives and for predictions of our future. The most ancient civilizations believed that dreams carried messages from the gods. Cuneiform tablets from Assyria and Babylon dating from the end of the fourth millennium BC depict a society whose priests and kings received warnings in their dreams from the deity Zaqar. *The Epic of Gilgamesh*, the great tale of a Mesopotamian hero-king written in the Akkadian language during the first millennium BC, is full of dream accounts, many replete with divine omens of danger or victory; in one a nightmare creature leads the hero Enkidu to the "Land of Dust" where the souls of the dead live in perpetual darkness.

Ancient Jewish tradition anticipated modern dream theory by recognizing that the life-circumstances of the dreamer are as important in interpretation as the dream content itself. The Babylonians revered the Jews as dream interpreters, and in the sixth century BC they summoned the Israelite prophet Daniel to interpret one of King Nebuchadnezzar's dreams, whereupon he correctly predicted the king's imminent seven years of madness (*Daniel* 4: 535). The Egyptians also prized the Israelites as dream interpreters. Joseph, sold into slavery in Egypt by his brothers, was able to rise from poverty to a position of considerable power by correctly interpreting the Pharaoh's dream that foretold seven plentiful and seven lean years in the ancient kingdom (*Genesis* 41: 138).

The Egyptians themselves did much to systematize dream interpretation during the years of the Middle Kingdom (2040-1786 BC), and their methods (as recorded in the Chester Beatty papyrus) have echoes in present-day dream directories. Dreams were understood in terms of meaningful opposites: thus, apparently happy dreams presaged disaster, while the worst nightmare could stand for better times to come. Individual dream symbols were fathomed either through rhyming similarities between word sounds, or through the modern method of association. It was believed that dreams contained messages from both good and evil spirits. By ingesting herbal potions or reciting spells, a dreamer would attempt to induce the good spirits and deter the bad. Thus prepared, the subject would sleep in the temple, and on awakening would submit his or her dreams to the temple priest for interpretation.

The ancient Greeks borrowed extensively from the Egyptians, and built more than three hundred shrines to serve as dream oracles. Mortals in these shrines were subjected to the soporific power of Hypnos, god of sleep, as he fanned them with his wings. Once they had passed into slumber, the god Morpheus could communicate with his adepts, passing warnings and prophecies to them in their dreams. Many of these shrines became famous as centres of healing. The sick would sleep there, hoping for a visitation from Aesculapius, the god of healing, who provided remedies for physical ills, sometimes effecting immediate cures, while the dreamer lay asleep surrounded by harmless yellow snakes. Aesculapius is also said to have summoned sacred snakes to the shrines to lick the wounds of the afflicted in their sleep, and so heal them. The *caduceus* – a device consisting of two snakes entwined around a rod – is still used to represent healing in Western symbolism.

Plato, writing in the fourth century BC, took a less mystical view, believing the liver to be the seat of dreams.

He attributed some dreams to the gods, but others to what in the *Republic* he called the "lawless wild beast nature which peers out in sleep", even in the sleep of the virtuous. While Plato thus anticipated Freud by more than 2,000 years, his pupil Aristotle foreshadowed twentieth-century scientific rationalism by arguing that dreams were triggered by purely sensory causes. Despite such cautionary voices, popular belief in the divinatory power of dreams remained widespread, and allegedly affected the course of Roman history: both Hannibal's epic journey across the Alps and Caesar's invasion of Rome were prompted by divine dream encouragement.

In the second century AD the Sophist philosopher Artemidorus of Daldis (who makes two brief and enigmatic appearances in Shakespeare's *Julius Caesar*) drew together the wisdom of earlier centuries, much of it already collected in the great library of the Babylonian King Asurna at Nineveh. His researches appeared in five highly influential dream books, the *Oneirocritica* (from the Greek *oneiros*, "a dream"). Although many of his interpretations sound quaint to present-day ears, Artemidorus was surprisingly modern in some respects. He identified the importance of the dreamer's personality in dream analysis, and observed the nature and frequency of sexual symbols. In his formulation that a mirror represents the feminine to men and the masculine to women, he even anticipated the Jungian concepts of the Anima and Animus (see page 38) .

Oriental dream traditions also offer many rewarding perspectives. Generally they are more philosophical and contemplative than Western traditions, and lay more emphasis upon the dreamer's state of mind than upon the predictive power of the dream itself. Chinese sages recognized that consciousness has different levels, and when interpreting dreams they took account of the physical condition and horoscope of the dreamer as well as of the time of year. They believed that consciousness leaves the body during sleep, and travels in various otherworldly realms: to arouse the dreamer abruptly, before mind and body are reunited, could be highly dangerous.

Indian *rsis*, or seers, also believed in the multi-layered nature of consciousness, recognizing the discrete states of waking, dreaming, dreamless sleep and *samadhi*, the bliss that follows enlightenment. A passage on dream interpretation in the *Atharva Veda*, a philosophical text dating from *c*.1,500-1,000 BC, teaches that in a series of dreams only the last is important: the suggestion is that dreams work progressively in solving problems or revealing wisdom. Hindu tradition also emphasizes the importance of individual dream images, relating them to a wider symbolic system incorporating the symbolic attributes of gods and demons. The Hindu belief that some symbols are universal while some are personal to the dreamer foreshadows the work of both Freud and Jung.

In the West, little progress was made in the study of dreams in the centuries after Artemidorus, as it was thought that he had made their mysteries plain. The Arabs, however, influenced by Eastern wisdom, continued to explore the dream world, producing dream dictionaries and a wealth of interpretations. Muhammad rose from obscurity to found Islam after a dream in which he received his prophetic call, and dreams afterwards came to the forefront of religious orthodoxy. In the *Koran*, the angel Gabriel comes to Muhammad in a dream, leading him on a silvery mare to Jerusalem and then up to heaven, where he meets Christ, Adam and the four apostles, enters the Garden of Delight and receives instructions from God.

The belief that dreams could be divinely inspired persisted during the early centuries of Christendom, and in the 4th century AD was part of the teaching of Church fathers such as St John Chrysostom, St Augustine and St Jerome. However, Christian orthodoxy was moving away from dream interpretation and prophecy. The dreams of the New Testament were seen as straightforward messages from God to the disciples and other founders of Christianity. Prediction also was redundant, because the future was believed to be in God's hands. By the Middle Ages, the Church even discounted the possibility of divine messages to the average believer, because God's revelation was only in and through the Church itself. The Dominican theologian Thomas Aquinas summed up the orthodox position of the thirteenth century when he advised that dreams should be ignored altogether. Martin Luther, who broke from the Roman Catholic Church to initiate the Protestant Reformation in the sixteenth century, taught that dreams, at most, simply showed us our sins.

However, dream interpretation was too strongly rooted in popular consciousness to be so readily dismissed. With the increasing availability of printed books in Europe from the fifteenth century onward, dream dictionaries proliferated, mostly based on the works of Artemidorus. Despite their naivety, such dictionaries filled a useful role in taking dream interpretation away from the seers and priests and placing it in the hands of the individual. And even though the scientific rationalists of the eighteenth century believed that dreams were of little consequence, and that their interpretation was a form of primitive superstition, at a popular level the interest in dreams gathered strength. Moreover, dreams began to feature as prominent themes in literature and art, as the new

Romanticism, led by visionaries such as William Blake and Goethe, rejected the claims of the rationalists and placed a new emphasis on the importance of the individual and the creative power of the imagination.

In nineteenth-century Europe even philosophers such as Johann Gottlieb Fichte (1762-1814) and Johann Friedrich Herbart (1776-1841) began to regard dreams as worthy of serious psychological study, and thus the way was prepared for the revolution in dream theory that began at the end of the century with Sigmund Freud (1856-1939). In 1899, in his mid-forties, Freud published his monumental work *The Interpretation of Dreams*. His studies as a neurologist had led him to search for the causes of neuroses in the unconscious mind, and after a lengthy course of self-analysis he became convinced of the role that dreams could play in providing access to these inner depths. For Freud the unconscious, or *id*, was primarily the seat of desires and impulses, mostly of a sexual nature, that are usually repressed by the conscious mind. Most dreams, he believed, are simple wish-fulfilments, or expressions of repressed ideas that force their way into our consciousness when our egos relax control during sleep. He argued that the function of dreaming is to preserve our sleep by preventing our wishes and desires from waking us up. Transformed into dream images and symbols, our deepest urges lose immediacy and so become more easily manageable. In Freud's terminology, these symbolic transformations are the manifest content of dreams, and he developed techniques in psychoanalysis to interpret the coded symbolism of this material to reveal what he called the latent content, which served as a key to the unconscious mind.

The Swiss-born psychologist Carl Jung (1875-1961) worked closely with Freud between 1909 and 1913, but found himself increasingly distanced by Freud's emphasis upon the underlying sexual content of dream symbols. Jung's views on dreams and on the operations of the mind in general form an important counterpoint (and, many psychologists would say, corrective) to those of Freud. More and more, Jung allowed the non-rational side of his nature (which had been powerfully expressed in his childhood fantasies and dreams) to emerge, and through a process of self-discovery, recorded by detailed note-taking, he came to develop his highly influential theory of the "collective unconscious" – the belief that the mind contains a vast internal reservoir of symbolism drawn upon by men and women, across all cultures, in their dreams and their deepest imaginings. Stored in the collective unconscious are the "archetypes" (see page 34), the profoundly resonating images and themes that inform the world's myths and religious and symbolic systems, as well as populating our most universally meaningful dreams.

Although many new techniques of dream interpretation have sprung up in recent times to supplement those pioneered by Freud and Jung, most draw heavily upon the work of the two masters whose theories of the unconscious and collective unconscious remain central to the most commonly held beliefs about the sources of our dreams. Psychoanalysis and Jungian analysis continue to be at the core of psychological investigation into dreams and their symbolic meaning.

The greatest breakthrough in dream research in the second half of the century was the discovery in 1953 of REM (Rapid Eye Movement) sleep, when the most vivid episodes of dreaming occur (see page 14). By waking sleepers up during REM periods, dream recall is greatly enhanced, enabling us to work more accurately with the images, symbols and other psychic events that punctuate our sleep.

However, much work remains to be done before we can construct a fully fledged science of dreaming. In the meantime, through dream workshops and other forms of analysis, we are building up a corpus of case studies that will, it is hoped, form an invaluable body of evidence for the dream scientists of the future.

Dreams and Sleep

We now know that probably everybody dreams. Although many of us forget most or all of the dreams that have visited us during the night, normally we dream for about one fifth of the time that we are asleep. Most of our "big" dreams come to us during REM, or Rapid Eye Movement, sleep, and are filled with narratives, symbols and detailed dream scenery. As we fall asleep and in the moments before we wake up, we experience the fleeting images of *hypnogogic* and *hypnopompic* dreams (see page 16). We dream at other phases of the night as well, and although some of these dreams are indistinguishable from REM dreams, most are fragmentary, less meaningful, less vivid, and rarely remembered upon waking.

Modern research into the physical patterns of dreaming began in 1953 with the work of American physiologist Nathaniel Kleitman and his student Eugene Aserinsky. In their "sleep laboratory" they observed that for short periods the eyes of sleeping infants move about rapidly behind closed eyelids. Subsequent research revealed that adults also manifest this phenomenon, and EEG readings, which record the electrical activity of the brain, showed that these periods of eye movement correspond with particular brain rhythms. The discovery of a link between eye movement and recognizable brain waves was a breakthrough in dream research, and this phase of sleep was termed REM (Rapid Eye Movement) sleep.

Further research revealed four distinct levels or stages of sleep, each characterized by particular physiological activities and brain rhythms. During the first fifteen minutes, the sleeper descends progressively through each of these stages, before spending about one hour in Stage 4, the deepest level, when the body is at its most relaxed and brain rhythms at their slowest. After this, an ascent back up to Stage 1 is often accompanied by a change in sleeping posture, and it is at this point that the first REM period of sleep begins, usually lasting for about ten minutes. Thereafter, the process of descent and ascent is repeated between four and seven times during the night, though sleep rarely again reaches a state as deep as Stage 4. Each REM episode becomes progressively longer, as does the frequency and rapidity of eye movement, and the final REM period can last as long as forty minutes.

REM sleep is also known as "paradoxical sleep", because during it brain activity, adrenaline levels, pulse rate and oxygen consumption come closest to those in wakefulness, yet muscle tone relaxes and the sleeper may prove particularly difficult to arouse. It is during REM sleep that most dreaming takes place. It seems that the physiological differences between REM sleep and the other three, deeper levels of sleep are as great as those between sleeping and waking. A number of American dream researchers have even suggested that REM sleep warrants recognition as a third basic form of human existence, seeming to confirm the ancient Hindu tradition that consciousness consists of three distinct levels: waking, dreamless sleep and dreaming.

In the 1960s researchers found that REM deprivation appears to lead to day-time irritability, fatigue, memory loss and poor concentration. Volunteers who were systematically deprived of REM sleep by being aroused whenever they entered the eye activity phase caught up on subsequent nights by engaging in more REM sleep than usual. If a subject is faced with total sleep deprivation, because of illness or other factors, the REM state has even been known to force its way into waking consciousness. It seems that we may badly need REM sleep, and this could be associated with a psychological need to dream.

Recent research has shown that dreams occurring during REM sleep are more visual in content than those that occur at other stages of sleep. Findings even indicate that the eye movements that take place in REM sleep may be synchronized with dream events, suggesting that the brain does not distinguish between the visual imagery of dreams and that of waking life. The same may be true of the brain's response to other dream sensations: certainly, stimuli such as a spray of water, a strong smell, a sudden sound such as the ringing of an alarm clock, a voice, a few notes of music, or a brief flash of light, may all be incorporated into a dream and "rationalized" in some way to fit in with its content.

Emotions may also be engaged. Heart rate and breathing often become erratic during REM sleep, gastric acid production may increase by as much as tenfold, asthmatics are more prone to attacks, and there is an increased tendency to cardiac arrest. Intriguingly, however, these extreme physiological changes do not necessarily have a direct relationship with reported dream content, but may instead result from what appears to be a total arousal of parts of the nervous system.

Yet however real such sensory experiences appear to be to the brain, something prevents us from performing in full the actions and emotions that fill our dreams. There is a general loss of muscle tone during REM sleep, and the eye muscles appear to be the only ones that are physically involved in acting out dream events. It has been shown that when dreams are at their most vivid, certain inhibitors are produced to prevent muscles from receiving the relevant impulses from the brain, thus ensuring that we do not act on sensory stimuli experienced in the dream. It is perhaps this effective paralysis that gives rise to the dream sensations of being unable to run, of attempting in vain to scream, or of trying to walk but being stuck in sand or water. The brain somehow prevents us from moving physically when asleep with the power and agility possessed by the dreaming mind.

Between Sleeping and Waking

Framing the vivid intensity of REM dreaming, our sleep begins and ends with dream images that visit the mind on the boundaries between sleep and wakefulness. Frederick Myers, one of the pioneer British explorers of the unconscious, gave the term *hypnogogic* to the dreams that precede sleep and *hypnopompic* to the dreams that come just as we are awakening.

As the dreamer falls asleep, the brain produces the steady alpha rhythms that characterize a state of deep relaxation; the pulse and breath rate slow down and the body temperature drops. Then the alpha rhythms begin to break up, and the sleeper enters fully into Stage 1 sleep where his or her mind is briefly filled with weird, hallucinatory dreams that characterize the hypnogogic state. Perhaps *visions* is a better word for them than dreams, for they lack both the narrative complexity and the emotional resonance of dreams encountered in deeper stages of sleep. When the Russian philosopher P.D. Ouspensky writes of "golden sparks and tiny stars … [which transform themselves] into rows of brass helmets belonging to Roman soldiers marching along the streets below", he is describing the extraordinary magical quality of hypnogogic dreams in which images seem to emerge and dissolve mysteriously into one another, establishing threads of association that would rarely occur to the waking mind.

Recent research on hypnogogia has centred on its visionary quality. As well as the characteristic scenery, objects and characters of REM type dreams, hypnogogic images include formless shapes such as waves of pure colour, designs and patterns often of perfect symmetry and geometrical regularity, and writing not only in the dreamer's mother tongue but in foreign, ancient and even entirely imaginary languages. Scrutinizing, archetypal faces swim in and out of view, comic and cartoon characters appear and disappear, and images are sometimes presented upside down, or reversed as if in a mirror.

Hypnopompic experiences share many of the characteristics of their hypnogogic counterparts and many actually briefly persist into wakefulness. René Descartes, the great French thinker hailed as the founder of modern philosophy, reported frequently seeing "sparks scattered around the room" as he emerged from sleep, while other writers speak of waking from hypnopompic dreams to see figures dancing around the bed or of finding an alien, surreal landscape stretching from their bedroom window. Many have also spoken of auditory rather than visual hallucinations in both hypnogogic and hypnopompic states. Voices warning of impending disaster, mysterious snatches of dialogue or bars of enchanting music are heard as clearly as if they come from within the room. Tactile and olfactory sensations are also common, and sometimes there is a complexity of awareness, as if the dreamer is simultaneously seeing a vision, listening in to a quite unconnected conversation, and smelling the sweet perfume of an invisible garden. It is hardly surprising that in ancient and medieval times many people believed that such experiences were glimpses of fairyland or visits from the gods.

Much recent research has attempted to explain the hallucinatory and sometimes trance-like nature of the hypnopompic and hypnogogic states by exploring the role that the ego plays as consciousness drifts between waking and sleep. It has been suggested that visionary hypnogogic dreams are a product of the ego's attempt to regain control over thought processes after the rapid change in

Through the window
A characteristic hypnopompic vision is that of a strange landscape stretching in front of the bedroom window, evoked here in a painting by David Hockney (Contrejour in the French Style, *1974*).

consciousness caused by the loss of contact with waking reality. For the American dream writer Van Dusen, however, hypnopompic and hypnogogic experiences are "the very antithesis of ego. Where ego is absent, ... [they] can appear". Hindu and Buddhist meditation orders teach that to reach a state of deep meditation, the adept must discard the ego on the way to self-enlightenment. Typically, as the adepts passed from one level of consciousness to another, they often saw visions, like those of hypnogogia, whose mysterious images and mandala-like designs served to encourage them in their quest.

The American psychologist Andreas Mavromatis suggested that both hypnopompic and hypnogogic experiences act as anxiety reducers, drawing the dreamer away from the trials and tensions of waking life, and thus serving to promote personal growth and development. By avoiding the narrative and emotional complexity of REM dreams and instead loosening the usual restrictions upon thought, they allow the dreamer to survey the contents of his or her unconscious, like leafing through the pages of an illustrated book. Thus, the dreamer experiences *at the level of awareness* the creative mental processes which usually stir in the depths of the unconscious. By comparing, contrasting and sorting the wealth of material stored in the mind, these processes engender creative insights which flash as if from nowhere into consciousness.

Lucid Dreaming

It was Jung who first put forward the evocative theory that we are dreaming all the time, and that it is only the distractions of waking life that leave us unaware of the fact. Recent research would seem to support him, demonstrating that the physical mechanisms of REM sleep are merely functionally inhibited during the day, probably because of a surfeit of other forms of stimulation. But there is another, even more intriguing body of evidence that seems to endorse Jung's theory. It relates to wakefulness in the midst of dreaming, or what is known as *lucid dreaming*.

The British dream researcher Celia Green has pinpointed several key differences between lucid and the much more usual non-lucid dreaming. Lucid dreams appear to be free from the irrationality and narrative disjointedness of the non-lucid state, and are sometimes seen and remembered with remarkable precision. During lucid dreams the dreamer may have access to all the memories and thought functions of waking life, and may feel no real difference between sleeping and waking. But above all, the dreamer is *aware that he or she is dreaming*.

Usually this awareness dawns abruptly. Something inaccurate or illogical in the scenery or events of a conventional dream can suddenly alert the dreamer to the fact of dreaming. The accompanying surge of excitement and an uncanny sensation of mind expansion make the experience unmistakable. Colours assume a vivid brightness, as if a veil has been stripped away, and objects stand out with an illuminated clarity that surpasses our perception of waking experience. Perhaps most remarkable is the dreamer's ensuing ability to control dream events, deciding where to go and what to do, and to experiment with the dreaming environment.

Yet intriguingly, however much power the dreamer may appear to have, he or she can never totally control the passage of a lucid dream. The decision, for example, to visit a tropical island in a dream may be the dreamer's own, but the island on arrival will prove every bit as novel and surprising as any seen for the first time in waking life. The Dutch physician William Van Eeden, who coined the phrase "lucid dreaming" in 1913, described the dream world as a "fake world, cleverly imitated but with small failures", and cited as an example a lucid dream in which he tried to break a claret glass that resisted all his efforts, but appeared broken when he saw it a few moments later, "like an actor missing his cue".

Some of the world's great religions have seen lucid dreaming in a mystical light. Hinduism and Buddhism assert that advanced adepts in the meditative arts retain consciousness throughout dreaming and dreamless sleep, and thus experience all their dreams as lucid. Israel Ragardie, a leading exponent of the Western mystery and alchemical traditions, wrote that an advanced practitioner "no longer passes the night in deep oblivion", but instead maintains a consistent level of consciousness so that "all is one continuous, free-flowing stream of awareness". Some esoteric teachings even suggest that seizing the initiative in dreams allows one to perform seemingly inexplicable acts in the waking world. Some Hindu mystics have claimed that adepts can appear at will in a number of places at the same time by practising dream control, then using this control first to visualize a place and then to visit it in a "dream body", visible and substantial to others.

In all cultures, and among initiates as well as adepts, the ability to control the events of a dream arises from a high degree of mental control in waking life. Instead of the unconscious working its Freudian mischief below the level of consciousness, or whispering its wisdom unheeded, in lucid dreaming the conscious and unconscious minds seem to establish effective communication and co-operation with each other. The lucid dream is their joint creation, and by increasingly bringing it under conscious control, the dreamer reaches deeper levels of self-knowledge.

By being aware of, and even dictating, the course of a dream, the dreamer can not only reach further into the unconscious mind, but may consciously decide to face the fears, desires and energies that reside there. Rather than running in panic from a dark and mysterious force or terrifying monster that inhabits the shadows at the edges of the dream world, lucid dreamers possess the control to summon such demons at will, then turn to confront them, aware that because they are only dreaming there is no real need for fear.

Once challenged, such forces usually lose their power, because in dreams as in waking life, the greatest fear is often fear itself. By confronting the demons in the unconscious, the dreamer not only lessens the terror that they are able to exert, but may also harness the energy of which he or she was previously afraid.

Allied to lucid dreaming, and perhaps a half-way house to it, is the sometimes disquieting dream experience known as *false awakening*. False awakening dreams are imbued with a vivid clarity similar to that of lucid dreams, yet the dreamer is not aware of dreaming, but believes that he or she is awake, and may dream in great detail of getting up, washing, having breakfast and setting off to work, only to wake up properly a little while later and have to repeat the whole process for real.

Lucid dreaming has been of valuable assistance to researchers trying to solve the problem of whether dream events occupy a normal time span or whether, as is popularly believed, they condense time. Findings by Stephen Laberge at the University of Stanford, California,

in which lucid dreamers carried out previously agreed eye movements to signify their progression through a series of pre-arranged dream events, suggests strongly that dream time approximates to real time. The dream may cut out irrelevant intervals that slow down waking life, but that is the only way that it manages to beat the clock.

Precognition and ESP

Belief in the predictive power of dreams is as old as written history. In many ancient cultures a dream that warned of impending flood, invasion, pestilence or the end of a ruling dynasty would be treated with the utmost solemnity and respect. Thus forewarned, a dreamer might succeed in averting the catastrophe by rescheduling the battle, arresting the palace spy or, like Noah, building an ark to survive the flood.

The legacy of European scientific rationalism has filled many of us today with a deep scepticism, yet stories of predictive dreaming remain relatively commonplace, especially with regard to the dreamer's own family or friends. But it was not until the work of John William Dunne that any consistent attempt to examine whether or not dreams can really provide glimpses into forthcoming events was published.

In 1902 Dunne, a British aeronautical engineer, had a dream that successfully foretold the eruption of Mount Pelée in Martinique. In his dream, he became convinced that the volcano was about to explode and hurried to warn the French authorities of the imminent catastrophe, telling them that 4,000 lives would be lost in the explosion. Subsequently he was amazed to read in a newspaper that the volcano had indeed erupted. The headlines, however, told of 40,000, not 4,000 deaths, and Dunne was later to conclude that it was not a vision of the volcano itself that had alerted him to the disaster, but a precognitive experience of reading the newspaper story and of misreading the headline that told of the number of deaths. The events of the dream, he thought, were simply a dramatization based upon the story that he had somehow seen in his dream.

A further series of precognitive dreams convinced Dunne that coincidence was no explanation for the frequency and sometimes detailed accuracy of his premonitions. He kept a dream diary for more than thirty years, recording his own dreams and those of his friends, to gather evidence for his increasingly radical ideas.

Dunne believed that dreams are able to make use of future events with the same freedom with which they select happenings from the past, wandering backward and forward through time, sometimes combining the past and future within the same dream. His book, *An Experiment with Time*, published in 1927, detailed an intricate and elaborate physical theory to account for this apparent flouting of scientific logic.

In 1971 two scientists, Montague Ullman and Stanley Krippner, working with the Maimonides Dream Laboratory team in New York, for the first time devised a method to investigate precognitive dreaming under laboratory conditions. They were able to work with Malcolm Bessant, a gifted English sensitive who had a strong history of precognitive dream experience. Before going to sleep, Bessant was told that he would be exposed to a "multi-sensory special waking experience" on the next day, chosen at random by the experimenters from a catalogue of dream items. He might be shown a fire, for example, or given some chocolate to eat while listening to a particular symphony. Researchers woke him up after each REM period to record what he had just dreamed and independent judges matched his dreams to the "special waking experiences" that followed them.

The degree of success that these experiments enjoyed is almost unparalleled in the history of parapsychology. Of the twelve projects that the Maimonides team completed between the years 1966 and 1972, nine yielded positive results, some of these at a very high level of significance.

During the course of the 1970s and 1980s, the Maimonides Dream Laboratory also carried out a number of experiments to test more general forms of ESP in dreams such as telepathy and clairvoyance, using famous art prints as targets. An "agent", located in a separate room or building from the subject, would concentrate upon one of these randomly chosen images in an attempt to "transmit" it to the dreamer and incorporate it into his or her dream. Again the results were highly impressive: psychologists declared an accuracy rate of 83.5 per cent for a series of 12 of these experiments, a finding against the odds of over a quarter of a million to one.

Researchers have collected a number of clairvoyant dreams apparently related to the sinking of the *Titanic*. Similarly, a retrospective appeal in the British press for dreams connected with the tragedy at Aberfan, a coalmining town in Wales where an avalanche of coal waste buried 140 people alive, produced impressive results that led to the establishment in 1967 of both the British Premonitions Bureau and the American Central Premonitions Registry.

Dreams of the death of loved ones, so-called farewell dreams, are even more common. One of the best-known was that of the explorer Henry Stanley, who after his capture at the battle of Shiloh during the American Civil War dreamed in detail of the unexpected death of his aunt some 4,000 miles away in Wales. Abraham Lincoln dreamed of his own death in 1865. In his dream, he wandered around a "death-like" White House following the far-off sounds of "pitiful sobbing". Every room was familiar and light, but there was no-one there. He finally entered the East Room to see a corpse laid out with its face covered, and wrapped in funeral vestments. When he asked the weeping mourners who was dead, he was told: "the President, he was killed by an assassin." A loud burst of grief from the crowd awoke him from his dream, and it was only a matter of days before the assassin John Wilkes Booth did indeed murder him.

But perhaps the most striking and strangest examples of clairvoyant and precognitive dreaming are those in which people without any knowledge of horse racing successfully predict race winners.

An electrical engineer and retired English civil servant named Harold Horwood developed the ability to consistently dream winners as an incidental result of intensive meditation practices, numbering among his successes many major events in the British racing calendar. Another successful dreamer was the Irish peer Lord Kilbracken, who over a short period dreamed nine winners and later became the racing correspondent of a leading London daily newspaper.

Dr Thelma Moss, an American dream researcher, includes among her collection of tipster dreams the remarkable case of a woman who dreamed up to four winners a week over a period of four months, while Montague Ullman reported a case of a man who dreamed the winners and runners-up of horse races on three successive nights.

Levels of Meaning

The interpretation of dreams must start from an understanding of the structure of the mind's various levels. The best model is still the four-fold hierarchy based upon the theories of Freud and Jung:

The conscious mind is governed by the *ego* – the "I" which can act in the outside world, and has a will. The conscious is the rational, self-aware aspect of the mind.

The preconscious contains material accessible to the conscious mind upon demand, such as facts, memories, ideas and motives.

The personal unconscious stores half-forgotten memories, repressed traumas and emotions, and unacknowledged motives and urges. This is what Freud called the *id*, which he saw as the primitive, instinctive side of ourselves, and which must be controlled by the ego.

The collective unconscious is a genetically inherited level of the mind containing what Jung called the "vast his-torical storehouse of the human race", a mental reservoir of ideas, symbols, themes and archtypes (see page 34) that form the raw material of many of the world's myths, legends and religious systems.

The first three levels were proposed by Freud, while the fourth was added by Jung. In accordance with this model, there are three main classes of dreaming, each one related to one of the three subconscious levels of the mind:

Level 1 is the most superficial class, drawing primarily upon material in the preconscious mind. Dream images from this level can often be taken at face value.

Level 2 deals with material from the personal unconscious, using predominantly symbolic language, much of it specific to the dreamer.

Level 3 contains what Jung called "grand dreams". These deal with material from the collective unconscious, operating only in symbols and archetypes.

The Nature of Dreaming

Are dreams a revelation from some profound creative source within ourselves, or the confused residue of thoughts and images left over from our waking life? Is the dreaming mind a window into the mysteries of the dreamer's deepest self, or a psychic garbage can containing random mental material that we would be wisest to ignore?

It is only in the West that we have made determined attempts to dismiss the value of our dreams. For all its advances in other directions, science has so far failed to come to a full understanding even of the theatre in which dreams are acted out – namely, sleep itself.

Since the discovery of REM, or Rapid Eye Movement, sleep in 1953 (see page 14), scientists have taken dreams into the laboratory, analyzing them with some of the aids of modern technology. Yet the question posed by Freud and Jung in the first half of the century remains largely unanswered: do we dream to preserve our sleep, or sleep so that we can dream?

Although scientists tend to agree that there must be a purpose to dreaming, they differ over what this purpose might be. The view to which most dream interpreters since the nineteenth century would subscribe is that dreams alert us to important aspects of the state of our unconscious minds.

Freud believed that dreams are coded messages devised by the unconscious to tell of the repressed desires and instincts that dwell there. Jungians go beyond this, recognizing a collective and creative sub-level (the collective unconscious: see page 23) that is vital to our well-being and generates not only the images of our dreams but also those of myth, legend and religious teachings. These theories are the twin cornerstones on which the ideas in this book are built.

Before going on to explore Freudian and Jungian theories in more depth, it is worth pausing to test the strength of the "psychic garbage" approach, which asserts that we dream to sort and discard our unwanted mental detritus in sleep, and that although the function of dreaming is important, the content of dreams is not.

Some scientists believe that the brain operates selectively, scrutinizing the mass of detail that bombards it during the wakeful hours, categorizing and storing relevant information, and dumping irrelevancies. According to this view, most of this processing takes place during the day, and much of the unwanted material is discarded immediately. The brain, however, also needs a period of consolidation when it can give its full attention to clearing the backlog, and this is what takes place during sleep. Scientists have compared this operation to a mainframe computer that goes "off line" during the night, and searches its files and programmes, modifying and updating them to take account of relevant new data and erasing or relegating to limbo any redundant or unwanted items. In dreams, however, fragments of the material being categorized and dumped emerge into sleeping consciousness, hopelessly jumbled together and beset by trains of unwanted associations. According to the "psychic garbage" theory, this mess of random images is what we dream.

There are several compelling objections to this approach. First, it is incorrect to claim that dream content is meaningless. Dreams have been shown to provide vital insights into both psychological and possibly physical health, and they can also be an invaluable aid to problem solving. Although they may appear at first to be confused and random, detailed analysis by an expert can show that they contain a wealth of meanings (sometimes ambivalent, but meanings nevertheless) related to the dreamer's circumstances. Lucid dreaming (see page 18) shows that far from the mind being "off line", full consciousness in dreaming is possible at times (and potentially at all times). There is no evidence that people who recall and work with their dreams are any less healthy psychologically than those who do not – in fact, the reverse seems to be true. Finally, although most dreams are indeed elusive in their signficance, some of them prove so memorable that years later they are as fresh in the mind as the major events of waking life.

"Garbage" theories of dreaming owed their genesis to the propensity of scientists for separating process from content. Such theories may seem feasible enough when the concern is only with the various neurophysiological aspects of dreaming, but they become untenable once proper attention is focused upon dream content itself.

No-one who maintains a dream diary (see pages 157 and 158) over a reasonable period of time should have any difficulty in recognizing that dreams have a remarkable coherence as a secret history of the self. Sadly, the belief of "garbage" theorists that dream recall is undesirable precludes them from studying the content of their own dreams, and leads them to disregard the very evidence that would discredit their ideas.

Yet if dreams do contain important messages from the unconscious to the conscious levels of the mind, why is it that we forget much of what we experience in sleep? There are several theories about this, one of which has to do with the manner of our waking. We no longer wake up suddenly as our primitive ancestors did, alert to the dangers of living in the open: instead, we emerge gradually from sleep in the safety of our beds, and it is possibly this which consigns most of our dreams to oblivion between sleeping and waking. Another theory is that we simply sleep too much, and the hours that we spend in dreamless sleep may smother the memories of our dreams. In dream workshops, people often report that their dream recall is greater than usual when away from home and in fresh surroundings, or when sleeping on a harder bed.

It may be that the cluttered, distracted and undisciplined nature of our minds also inhibits dream recall. Adepts of the Hindu and Buddhist esoteric orders, and certain followers of the Western mystery tradition, are said to enjoy unbroken consciousness throughout their sleep, largely as a consequence of their intensive training in techniques of concentration and meditation. They claim to remember their dreams because they are not only conscious of them while they are taking place but also in control of the direction that they take.

The classic theory of dream amnesia, however, is that advanced by Sigmund Freud, who believed that the main reason that we forget our dreams is because they are often too painful to remember. According to Freud, dream amnesia has nothing to do with incidental aspects of the dreamer's lifestyle, but is directly caused by what he called the *censor*, a repressive ego defence mechanism that protects the conscious mind from the mass of disturbing images, instincts and desires that inhabit the depths of the unconscious.

Dream research is one of the few remaining areas where the layperson is as competent as the professional. It requires no equipment beyond a notebook and pencil for writing down dreams, an alarm clock for those who have difficulty with dream recall, some guidance on dream interpretation, and the necessary level of motivation and perseverance. Armed with these minimal resources, all of us can explore deeper and deeper into our dream life, and reach our own conclusions as to the function and value of dreams in our life as a whole.

Freud on Dreams

Sigmund Freud (1856-1939) began his classic work *The Interpretation of Dreams* with what was for 1899 a revolutionary statement: "I shall bring forward proof that there is a psychological technique which makes it possible to interpret dreams." Modern dream psychology was born in this sentence.

The Interpretation of Dreams sold only 351 copies in the first six years, but eventually ran through numerous editions, and became one of the very few books to have changed our way of looking at ourselves.

Freud was born in Freiburg in Moravia (now in the Czech Republic), and trained in Vienna as a medical doctor under the noted neurophysiologist Ernst Brücke. From Brücke, Freud derived his deterministic belief that all living phenomena are determined by the laws of cause and effect, a view which later predisposed him to recognize dreams as subject to these same laws.

Later, while working in Paris with the famous neurologist and medical hypnotist J.M. Charcot, he concluded that neuroses are caused by psychological rather than by physiological factors, and on his return to Vienna he developed (partly with the help of psychiatrist Josef Breuer) the technique of free association for identifying what these factors might be.

The results of this work with free association convinced him that many of them lie below the level of the conscious mind, and are associated with the emotional damage caused in early childhood by the repressions and distortions of the life instinct, specifically of the sexual urge, in response to the need for social and parental approval.

Recognizing that this revealed the crucial importance of the unconscious, Freud then undertook a lengthy course of self-analysis in order to explore further this area of the mind, and as a result of his discoveries he became convinced of the role that dreams can play in providing access to material hidden there.

Freud famously described dreams as "the royal road to the unconscious", and firmly believed that he had unravelled their full mystery. Many of his conclusions are now disputed, but we owe him a profound debt for recognizing the questions that we should be asking about the meaning and purpose of dreaming, and about the insights dreams give us not only into the contents of the unconscious but also into the role that the unconscious plays in our mental life as a whole.

Underlying Freud's understanding of dreams was his belief that the mind processes its material at different levels. His study of his own dreams, and those of his patients, led him to distinguish between what he called the

"primary process" which operates in the unconscious, dreaming mind, and the "secondary process" that characterizes conscious thought.

The former process differs from the latter in that it lacks organization and coordination, and consists only of instinctive impulses, each pressing toward its own fulfilment. Freud believed that the primary process takes unconscious impulses, desires and fears, and turns them into symbols; these are linked by associations that have no regard for categories such as time and space, or right and wrong, as the unconscious is unaware of the logic, values and social adaptations of conscious life.

The secondary process, on the other hand, works by subjecting thoughts to the laws of logic, like a sentence that is governed by the rules of grammar.

Freud maintained that unconscious instincts dwell in a kind of primitive chaos, each seeking gratification independently of the others, and in an animalistic and amoral way. He used the term *id* (literally, "it") to describe the primary part of the mind, and argued that it contains "everything that is inherited … [and] is present at birth" – in other words, that it contains the primordial instincts that have motivated us since the beginnings of the human race, specifically the instincts for self-survival and for the survival of the species.

In Freud's view, the id dominates unconscious life, and dreams are the acting out in fantasy form, or the *wish-fulfilment*, of its desires and energies. Yet dreams do not emerge directly from this mass of anarchic instincts. If they did, they would arouse the dreamer with their disturbing, often antisocial, and potentially psychologically harmful content. Hence, they express themselves only in symbolic form (as will shortly be more fully explained).

In waking life the ego, the rational part of the mind that is grounded in commonsense reality, and adheres to an acquired moral sense, keeps the id's primitive urges at bay. In sleep, however, the ego relaxes its conscious control, and the id comes to the fore, flooding our mind with its mischievous agenda.

To protect the sleeping ego from being disturbed by this inundation to the point where the dreamer is actually awoken, a mental device that Freud termed the censor struggles to translate the id's material into a less disruptive form. The purpose of dreaming is therefore to preserve sleep by symbolizing dream content in a way that renders it innocuous to the censor. Dreams thus operate in much the same way as neurotic symptoms, which preserve an equilibrium in the ego by striving to allow potentially overwhelming anxieties and instincts to be expressed in a form which it can handle.

Much recent criticism of Freud's ideas has centred upon the hierarchical aspect of his view of the mind. Freud believed that "secondary" functions such as rationality, morality and the role of the ego are developed only after the "primary" wishes and instincts of the unconscious have been tamed and repressed, as if learning depends on a child's ability to beat his or her way through the dark forest of primary processes in order to reach the open, daylit clearing of the conscious ego. Later research suggests that it is more likely that there is no such struggle in the mind between primary and secondary processes, and that rather than continually competing with each other they in fact coexist as partners.

For Freud, dreams always have a *manifest* and a *latent* content. The manifest content is what the dream appears to be saying, often a jumble of apparent nonsense, while the latent content is what the unconscious is really trying to communicate to consciousness.

The manifest content has two major methods of disguising latent content in a way that can evade the censor. The first is *condensation*: the fusing of two or more dream images to form a single symbol. For example, Freud often interpreted images of older men in his patients' dreams as a condensation of their fathers, on the one hand, and of Freud himself, their analyst, on the other. Working by association rather than by logical connections, the manifest content amalgamates the two images to reflect a similarity in our attitudes toward them both.

The second major device used by the dreaming mind is *displacement*. Like condensation, displacement works by association, translating one dream image into another, rather in the way that metaphor works in language. When one of Freud's patients dreamed of a ship in full sail, its bowsprit jutting out before it, Freud had no difficulty in interpreting this as a displacement image, the ship standing for his patient's mother, the sails representing her breasts and the bowsprit symbolizing the penis that his patient always imagined his forceful mother to have.

Free association was the method developed by Freud to bypass the condensations and displacements of manifest content in order to arrive at an interpretation of dreams. By following the chains of free association that start from an individual dream image, either we continue wherever our train of thought leads us, or we suddenly stop when we meet resistance, a sudden blockage in the mind that usually reveals the nature of the unconscious problem.

Whatever the outcome, the process enables us to join the "royal road" that leads to the instincts and desires buried in the id, which Freud thought were the sources of our dreams.

Another important idea in Freud's interpretative method is *secondary revision*. This term describes the way in which we alter the events and images of our dreams either when recounting them to someone else or when trying to remember them ourselves. A Freudian psychoanalyst would look for clues in the way in which a patient might "revise" his or her dreams, lending them greater internal consistency and coherence than they in fact possess.

Freud's theory that all dreams originate from the primal chaos of the id was strongly opposed by those who subscribed to the increasingly widespread belief that dreams may be simply a continuation of the mind's daytime thoughts, or reactions to events that recently took place in waking life.

Accordingly, in the 1920s, following disagreements with Jung and other psychologists working on the origin and meaning of dreams, Freud modified his views in order to draw a distinction between what he called dreams from "above" and those from "below". Dreams from below arise from the unconscious and "may be regarded as inroads of the repressed into waking life", while those from above result from the day's events, "reinforced [by] repressed material that is debarred from the ego" [that is, material unacceptable to the ego, and thus repressed in the id].

Freud believed that much of our conscious behaviour is also prompted by the need to satisfy unconscious urges. As we go about the business of the day, we channel instinctive energy into socially acceptable forms, using such *ego defence* mechanisms as repression, denial and projection in order to keep painful material out of conscious awareness. The ego continually strives to placate the id, to persuade it that its drives are not going unheard by consciousness as a whole. If the ego should fail in this task of placation, or of maintaining its defences against the id's more disturbing onslaughts, the pent-up instincts and buried traumas of the unconscious can break through into our conscious minds, leading to full-scale mental breakdown.

Even if we escape such a fate, we may waste a great deal of our energy in conflicts between the ego and the id, leading to the obsessions, depressions and anxieties that constitute neurosis.

However, with the help of a psychoanalyst who can coax the content of the id carefully into consciousness, where it can be seen and understood for what it is, we can avoid such conflicts and strip the id of much of its power. Freud saw the interpretation of dreams as essential to this task.

Jung on Dreams

Jung is often regarded as an early and ardent disciple of Freud who eventually decided to part company with him. In fact, Jung was already well on the way to developing his own theories before he met Freud in 1907, and although he continued to pay generous tribute to the older man after their rift in 1913, there was a measure of scientific disagreement between them from the start.

Carl Gustav Jung (1875-1961), the founder of analytical psychology, was born near Basel in Switzerland, and after qualifying as a medical doctor at the local university spent most of his life in private psychotherapeutic practice at Kusnacht on Lake Zurich. Like Freud, with whom he worked closely from 1909 to 1913, he believed in the role that the unconscious plays in neurosis and psychosis, and in the important part played by dreams in uncovering the sources of unconscious problems.

Jung departed from Freud, however, in his realization that the common themes running through the delusions and hallucinations of his patients could not all emerge from their personal unconscious conflicts, but must stem from some common source. His extensive knowledge of comparative religion, mythology and symbol systems such as alchemy convinced him that similar common themes run across cultures and across the centuries, and thus was born his belief in the collective unconscious, a genetic myth-producing level of the mind common to all men and women, and serving as the well-spring of psychological life. Jung gave the term "archetypes" to the mythological motifs and primodial images that emerge from the collective unconscious, and saw these as making symbolic appearance over and over again in the great myths and legends of the world, and in our deepest and most meaningful dreams.

Ernest Jones, Freud's biographer, writes of Jung's "tendency to occultism, astrology, and ... mysticism", but makes it clear that the ultimate reason for Jung's break-up with Freud was his rejection of Freud's insistence that life energy is primarily sexual. The implications of this disagreement for dream interpretation were profound. Jung saw the sexual symbolism that emerged in dreams as symbolic in turn of a deeper, non-sexual level of meaning, while Freud chose to interpret the sexual content literally. For Jung, "grand" dreams (that is, those stemming from the collective unconscious) were not coded messages alluding to particular desires, but gateways to a mythic world, "the vast historical storehouse of the human race".

Jung also differed from Freud in his method of exploring the unconscious through dream interpretation. Rejecting Freudian free association, he favoured instead the technique of direct association. Jung criticized Freud's method because it allows the mind to freewheel, following a chain of association that leads away from the original dream image and often ends up in some far distant place. Through direct association, Jungians concentrate upon the dream itself, preventing the client's train of thought from wandering by returning it again and again to the original image. Jung conceded that free association leads to valuable psychological insights, but thought that these insights often bear no connection with the message contained in the dream. One might as well take a word at random from the dictionary, and use that as a starting-point.

For Jung, psychotherapy is not a quest to discover the dark secrets of our past by delving into childhood traumas, but a process of discovery and self-realization. Jungians believe that by being in touch with the mythic themes of our collective unconscious, we gradually integrate the disparate and sometimes conflicting aspects of our selves, developing our full potential as we pass through life's successive stages.

Whereas Freud tried to narrow down his dream interpretations by approaching them with rigid theoretical presuppositions, Jung favoured the *amplification* of dream symbols, drawing out their deeper meanings by placing them in their wider mythic and symbolic contexts.

Jung's exhaustive analysis of dream material revealed "the numerous connections between individual dream symbolism and medieval alchemy". Alchemy was not merely a mystical forerunner of modern chemistry, but a precursor of the modern study of the unconscious, and of techniques for transforming the dross, or base matter, of psychic conflict and confusion into the gold of personal wholeness.

Jung saw alchemy as a powerful undercurrent to Western religion and philosophy much "as the dream is to consciousness, and just as the dream compensates the conflicts of the conscious mind, so alchemy endeavours to fill in the gaps left open by the Christian tension of opposites".

Jung not only drew parallels between dream symbols and their alchemical counterparts, but also found in alchemy a symbolic representation of the very process of Jungian analysis and the development of the human psyche. In their search for the powers of self-transformation, alchemists strove to unify opposites such as white and black, sulphur and mercury, heat and cold, sun and moon, life and death, male and female, thus creating the Philosopher's Stone, the single unifying principle that also served as a source for certain of the myths surrounding the Holy Grail.

Jung found in these symbolic alchemical transformations a complex metaphor for the union of male and female, Anima and Animus, conscious and unconscious, matter and spirit that that in his view led to wholeness within the human psyche itself – a process described by Jung, borrowing an alchemical term, as *individuation*.

With his emphasis on the importance of present experience (in contrast to Freud's preoccupation with childhood), Jung saw each stage of life as carrying developmental significance, and stressed the capacity for growth and self-actualization even into advanced old age. The aim of psychotherapy, and thus of dream analysis, was to give the individual access to the personal and collective unconscious, not in order to learn the dark secrets of the past, but to discover and integrate each aspect of the self into psychic wholeness. In the course of such integration, men and women reconcile not only hitherto conflicting sides of themselves, but free an often repressed *religious function*. Jung discovered through his work with the dreams and neuroses of his clients that this function is at least equal in strength to the Freudian instincts of sex and agression. The religious function has nothing to do with creeds and dogmas, but is an expression of the collective unconscious that inspires us toward spirituality and love.

CASE FILE I

*Freud had this famous dream in 1895, and it was the first that he submitted
to detailed interpretation. It concerned Irma, a young widow and family
friend whom Freud was treating for "hysterical anxiety".*

The dream: Freud dreamed that he received Irma and other guests in a large hall. He took her to one side and reproached her for rejecting his "solution" to her anxiety problems: "if you still get pains, it's really only your fault". She complained bitterly of "choking" pains in her throat, stomach and abdomen. Alarmed, Freud examined her throat, in case he had missed an organic cause for her problems, and found a large white patch as well as "some remarkable curly structures", similar to "bones of the nose". Dr M. repeated the examination and confirmed Freud's findings. Freud decided that the infection was caused by an injection, administered by Otto, a doctor of his acquaintaince, probably with an unclean syringe. In Dr M.'s opinion, Irma would soon contract dysentery and the toxin would be eliminated.

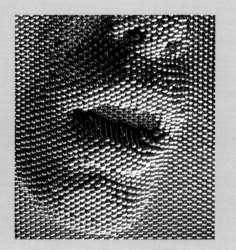

The interpretation: While carrying out a "detailed analysis" of the dream, subjecting key parts of it to free association, Freud became aware that it was a wish-fulfilment, "a particular state of affairs as I should have wished it to be". In the dream, Freud first blames Irma for her own pains. His feeling that the causes may be organic represents both his hidden wish to escape responsibility for the failure of psychoanalysis, and his fear that he has been confusing psychosomatic and physical problems. He concludes that "I was not responsible for Irma's pains, but that Otto was. Otto had in fact annoyed me by his remarks about Irma's incomplete cure, and the dream gave me my revenge by throwing the reproach back on him". In Freud's wish-fulfilling dream world, Irma's "pains" were not caused by his handling of her psyche but by an unclean syringe Otto had used when giving her an injection.

Freud's anxiety about his own treatment of Irma was symbolized by the part played by Dr M., to whom Freud had once made an appeal when his own unwitting mistreatment of a patient had led to her fatal illness. The white patch on Irma's throat reminded him of diphtheria and of the distress caused when his own daughter had the disease; while the nasal-like bones recalled his worries over his own use of cocaine, a practice discouraged by his medical peers, and one which had led to the death of a close friend.

Freud's interpretation indciates the varied and complex meanings which may be carried by a single dream. Concern that he was not to blame for her pains, resentment toward Otto for questioning his treatment of her, his own misgivings over the treatment, remembered anxieties over his daughter, and his worries over his use of cocaine, all feature at some point.

CASE FILE II

Jung had this dream when was trying to establish a relationship between archetypal dream symbols arising from the collective unconscious and the medieval symbolic system of alchemy.

The dream: Jung had had a series of recurrent dreams in which a new wing had been added to his house. He had never been able to enter it until one night he passed through the double doors into the wing and found himself in a zoological laboratory resembling his dead father's workroom. Surrounding him were hundreds of species of fish preserved in bottles. He saw a curtain billowing and sent someone to see if there was a window open, and the person returned in terror to say that there was "something haunted" behind the curtain. Jung went to look and found his dead mother's bedroom, empty except for rows of what seemed like small floating pavilions, each housing two beds. He knew at once that this was where his mother kept pairs of spirits. A door opened into a vast hall like the lobby of a hotel, decorated with pillars, small tables and sumptuous hangings, in which a brass band played loud tunes and marches. The jollity and worldliness were quite at odds with the sombre atmosphere of the first two rooms that Jung had entered.

The interpretation: Many of Jung's "grand" dreams took place in a dream house, identifiably his own yet strangely different. By finally gaining access to a new wing in his house, he was symbolically entering areas of his mind that had previously remained unexplored, but which his recent studies of alchemy were opening to him.

The wing consisted of two distinct parts. The laboratory and bedroom in which he found himself represented what Jung called "a dwelling of the night", the hidden spiritual side of himself further symbolized by the many fish, an ancient symbol of Christ. Beyond the curtains, where his own Shadow (page 37) potentially lurked, the bedroom contained mysteriously floating pairs of beds that served as symbols of the alchemical *coniunctio*, the mystical wedding within the self of male and female that leads to inner wholeness. The second part of the wing, consisting of the hall with its loud band and ostentatious furniture, represented the conscious mind, the rational world of daylight.

By amplifying the major symbols of the dream, Jung established associations with the myth of the Holy Grail. His father had been a pastor, a "fisher of men", and Jung recognized in him the figure of the wounded Fisher King, an archetypal symbol in the Grail legend of the suffering we experience through ignorance of our true spiritual nature. By confronting his fear of the Shadow, and passing beyond the haunted curtain, Jung had found in the alchemical *conjunctio* the very symbol he had been seeking to connect the grand themes of dreams and those of the great myths. In the coming together of conscious and unconscious, the male and female sides of the self, we find our spiritual nature and heal the suffering of the Fisher King.

The Language of Archetypes

Archetypes are the common themes, or in Jung's words "mythological motifs", that emerge from the collective unconscious and reappear in symbolic form again and again in myths, symbol systems and dreams. James Hillman, the contemporary (American) founder of archetypal psychology, refers to them as "the deepest patterns of psychic functioning": they are "the roots of the soul governing the perspectives we have of ourselves and the world … the axiomatic, self-evident images to which psychic life and our theories about it ever return".

Without access to the myth-making vitality of the archetypes, we are confined to a few rooms of the splendid mansion that is the mind, and shut out from the creative source of our own psychic life.

In most instances, archetypal dreams leave us feeling that we have received wisdom from a source outside what we commonly recognize as ourselves. Whether we describe this source as a reservoir of spiritual truth or as an untapped dimension of our own minds is of less importance than that we acknowledge its existence.

In our "grand" dreams, archetypes appear as symbols, or take personified form as the particular gods and goddesses, heroes and heroines, fabulous beasts and powers of good and evil, that are most familiar to our conscious minds. Jungians stress, however, that we should never identify with individual archetypes, because each is only a fragment of the complete self. By integrating the many archetypes of the collective unconscious, Jungians hope to progress towards individuation (see page 31).

Archetypal dreams are most likely to occur at important transitional points in life, such as early schooldays, puberty, adolescence, early parenthood, middle age, the menopause, and old age. They also occur at times of upheaval and uncertainty, and mark the process toward individuation and spiritual maturity.

Jung found archetypal dreams occurring in all walks of life, experienced as much by "people who are inwardly cut off from humanity and oppressed by the thought that nobody else has their problems" as by those far advanced on the individuation process. Yet in these two extreme cases the dream content is different: the dreams of the alienated personality reflect personal concerns and the dreams of the integrated personality reflect supra-personal themes such as birth and death, immortality, and the meaning of existence.

However, Jung cautions that if archetypal dreams contain potent material that appears greatly to contradict the ideas and beliefs of the dreamer's conscious mind, or that lacks the moral coherence of genuine mythological material, then a deep division, born of resistance and repression, may exist between the collective unconscious and the dreamer's waking life. Such psychic blocks must be dealt with before further progress is possible.

Dream archetypes are vital to the search for our "true selves". By looking out for them in dreams, and learning to recognize them, we can build bridges that stretch over to our unconscious minds. Each archetype is a link in a chain of mythic associations. By identifying one archetype, we can draw other archetypes into dreaming awareness, and so delve deeper into the creative power of our collective unconscious.

According to the Jungian analysts Edward Whitmont and Sylvia Perera, we know that we have entered the world of archetypes if our dreams confront us with elements that are rationally impossible in everyday life, and that lead us to "the realms of myth and magic". Most dreams reflect the constraints of waking reality, but the moment that we find ourselves in a shape-shifting world in which animals talk, men rise unscathed from mortal wounds, strangers enter through locked doors, and trees twine themselves into beautiful women, we know that we are in the presence of archetypal powers.

Archetypal dream images and events often appear to have a predetermined, all-encompassing, dramatic power, described by Whitmont and Perera as a "numinosity which creates a sense of awe in the dreamer". The dream may be set in an historical or cultural environment far removed from that of the dreamer, symbolizing the fact that he or she is travelling outside the boundaries of waking sensory and psychological experience. It has also been found that archetypal dreams convey a sense of great significance to the dreamer, prompting him or her to see in them "some suggestion of enlightenment, warning, or supernatural help". Above all, archetypal dreams have about them what Jung called a "cosmic quality", a sense of temporal or spatial infinity conveyed by dream experiences such as movement at tremendous speed over vast distances, or a comet-like flight through space, an experience of hovering far above the earth, or a breathtaking expansion of the self until it transcends its narrow individuality and embraces all of creation. Cosmic qualities can also emerge in our dreams as astrological or alchemical symbols, or as experiences of death and re-birth.

Many archetypal dreams involve magical journeys or quests which often, like the quest for the Holy Grail, represent a search for some aspect of ourselves. A common theme in fairy tales is that of the young hero who must journey to a foreign land to discover his manhood, or true self, before returning to slay a dragon, or rescue a suffering maiden. When such themes appear in dreams they usually symbolize a journey into the unconscious, where the dreamer seeks to find and assimilate fragmented parts of the psyche in order to achieve a psychological confidence and wholeness that can differentiate him or her from collective society.

A common archetypal journey is the *night sea passage*, in which the hero is swallowed up and nearly destroyed by the monster that he has attempted to slay. As in the Biblical tale of Jonah and the whale, the hero still manages to destroy the monster from within, to escape and finally to reach land in a symbolic representation of the dreamer's successful quest to reclaim life-energy from the depths of the unconscious, and thus deprive unconscious impulses of the power to dominate conscious behaviour.

Other archetypal journeys, such as sea voyages toward the rising sun, can represent re-birth and transformation. Dreams may also involve baptism and other forms of ritual initiation, emergence from the primal depths of a cave, or alchemical archetypes such as the phoenix rising from the flames that destroy the past and leave the dreamer free to create his or her future. Such mythical creatures as the phoenix may not embody primary archetypes in themselves, but may be used by the dreaming mind as representatives of the archetypes. For example, sphinxes in dreams may symbolize the occult wisdom of the archetype of the Great Mother, while the Hindu deity Garuda (half man, half eagle) may stand for the fierce, purifying energy of the Wise Old Man. Jung saw the Dragon, however, as a primary symbol, related to the collective or overbearing social aspect of the Great Mother, who must be slain if the hero is to be free.

One archetype with a profoundly numinous quality is the Spirit, the opposite of matter, sometimes manifested in dreams as an impression of infinity, spaciousness, invisibility. The Spirit may also appear as a ghost, or as a visit from the dead, and its presence often indicates a tension between the material and non-material worlds. Other major archetypes, including the Shadow, the Trickster and the Divine Child, are described on the following pages.

Seven Major Archetypes

The Wise Old Man

The Wise Old Man (or Woman) is what Jung called a *mana* personality, a symbol of a primal source of growth and vitality which can heal or destroy, attract or repel. In dreams this archetype may appear as a magician, doctor, professor, priest, teacher, father, or any other authority figure, and by its presence or teachings convey the sense that higher states of consciousness are within the dreamer's grasp. However, like the wizard or the shaman, the *mana* personality is only quasi-divine, and can lead us away from the higher levels as well as toward them. Jung himself enjoyed a life-long relationship with a *mana* personality of his own: he called him Philemon, and frequently passed his days talking and painting with him.

The Trickster

The Trickster is the archetypal antihero, the "ape of God", a psychic amalgam of the animal and the divine. Jung likened him to the alchemical Mercurius, the shape-shifter, full of sly jokes and malicious pranks. Sometimes seen as an aspect of the Shadow, the Trickster appears in dreams as a clown or buffoon, who while mocking himself at the same time mocks the pretensions of the ego and its archetypal projection, the Persona. He is in addition the sinister figure who disrupts our games, exposes our schemes, and spoils our dream pleasure. The Trickster, like the Shadow, is also a symbol of transformation: he is indestructible, changing his shape and disappearing and re-appearing at will. He often turns up when the ego is in a dangerous situation of its own making, through vanity, over-arching ambition or misjudgment. He is untamed, amoral, and anarchic.

The Persona

The Persona is the way in which we present ourselves to the outside world – the mask that we adopt in order to deal with waking life. Useful and non-pathological in itself, the Persona becomes dangerous if we identify with it too closely, mistaking it for the real self. It can then appear in our dreams as a scarecrow or a tramp, or as a desolate landscape, or as social ostracization. To be naked in dreams often represents loss of the Persona.

The Shadow

Jung defines the Shadow as "the thing a person has no wish to be". Everything substantial casts a shadow, and for Jung the human psyche is no exception: "unfortunately there can be no doubt that Man is, on the whole, less good than he wants or imagines himself to be". Jung identified the shadow as the primitive, instinctive side of ourselves. The more that we repress this side, and isolate it from consciousness, the less chance there is of preventing it from bursting "forth suddenly in a moment of unawareness". Even at best, "it forms an unconscious snag, thwarting our most well-meant intentions".

Jung credited Freud with drawing proper attention to this "abyss in human nature". Concealed under our civilized veneer, the Shadow reveals itself in the selfish, violent and often brutal actions of individuals, communities and nations. It feeds on greed and fear and can be projected outward as the hate that persecutes and makes scapegoats of minority groups. In dreams, the Shadow usually appears as a person of the same sex, often in a threatening, nightmarish role. Because the Shadow can never be totally eliminated, it is often represented by dream characters who are impervious to blows and bullets, and who pursue us past every obstacle, and into the blind alleyways and eerie basements of the mind. However, it can also take the form of the brother or sister figure (the Biblical figure of Cain), or the stranger who confronts us with the things we prefer not to see and the words we prefer not to hear.

Because the Shadow is obsessional, autonomous and possessive, it arouses in us strong emotions of fear, anger or moral outrage. Yet Jung insists it is not evil in itself, merely "somewhat inferior, primitive, unadapted and awkward". Its appearance in dreams indicates a need for a more conscious awareness of its existence, and for more moral effort in coming to terms with its dark energies, which otherwise prey upon and gradually overpower the conscious mind.

The Shadow does things in "the old way", as Jung put it; and we must learn to accept and integrate it because the unpalatable messages it gives us are often indirectly for our own good.

The Divine Child

The Divine Child is the archetype of the regenerative force that leads us toward individuation: "becoming as a little child", as it is expressed in the Gospels. It is therefore the symbol of the true self, of the totality of our being, as opposed to the limited and limiting ego which is in Jung's words "only a bit of consciousness, and floats upon an ocean of the (hidden) things". In dreams, the Divine Child usually appears as a baby or infant. It is both innocent and vulnerable, yet at the same time inviolate and possessed of vast transforming power. Contact with the child can strip us of the sense of personal aggrandisement upon which the ego so greedily feeds, and reveal to us how far we have strayed from what once we were and aspired to be.

The Anima and Animus

Jung's studies and clinical experience convinced him that we each carry within us the whole of human potential, male and female. The Anima represents the "feminine" qualities of moods, reactions and impulses in man, and the Animus the "masculine" qualities of commitments, beliefs and inspirations in woman. More importantly, as the "not-I" within the self, the Anima and Animus serve as *psychopompi*, or soul guides, to the vast areas of our unacknowledged inner potential.

Mythology represents the Anima as maiden goddesses or women of great beauty, such as Athena, Venus and Helen of Troy; while the Animus is symbolized by noble gods or heroes, such as Hermes, Apollo and Hercules. If Anima or Animus appear in our dreams in these exalted forms, or as any other powerful representation of man or woman, it typically means that we need to integrate the male and female within us. If ignored, these archetypes tend to be projected outward into a search for an idealized lover, or unrealistically ascribed to partners or friends. If we allow them to take possession of our unconscious lives, men can become over-sentimental and over-emotional, while women may show ruthlessness and obstinacy. However, once the process of individuation has begun, these archetypes serve as guides, taking the dreamer deeper and deeper into the realm of inner possibilities.

The Great Mother

The image of the Great Mother plays a vital role in our psychological and spiritual development. Its prevalence in dreams, myths and religion is derived not only from our personal experiences of childhood, but also from the archetype of all that cherishes and fosters growth and fertility on the one hand, and all that dominates, devours, seduces and possesses on the other.

Not only is the energy of the Great Mother divine, ethereal and virginal, but it is also chthonic (generated from the earth) and agricultural: the earth mother was worshipped as the bringer of harvests. Always ambivalent, the Great Mother is an archetype of feminine mystery and power who appears in many forms: at her most exalted as the queen of heaven, at her most consuming as the Sumerian goddess Lilith, the gorgon Medusa, or the witches and harpies prevalent in myth and folktale.

For Freud, however, the symbolic dream mother was far more a representation of the dreamer's relationship with his or her own mother than an abstract archetype. Freud observed in fact that most dreams involve three people – the dreamer, a woman and a man – and that the theme that most commonly links the three characters is jealousy. Freud believed that the dream woman and dream man most represent the dreamer's mother and father, and maintained that they symbolize aspects of the Oedipus and Electra complex from which men and women respectively suffer. (In Greek myth Oedipus, unaware of his actions, slew his father and married his mother: Freud saw this as symbolizing the early male sexual desire for the mother, and jealousy of the father. Electra, similarly, desired her father and was jealous of her mother.)

CASE FILE III

The dreamer is a university professor. He is currently trapped between maintaining his considerable academic reputation, and risking it by openly declaring his growing interest in mysticism and spiritual growth.

The dream: "I had been swimming in the sea, and went to stand under a freshwater shower higher up the beach. The water ran over my back, but before I could rinse my front, I had to make way for other people. I started to protest but suddenly found myself in a smart drawing-room still in my bathing suit and dripping water on the carpet. There were several middle-aged well-dressed women there who looked at me disapprovingly, and a much younger one standing with a mandolin who said: 'Don't worry, music can always dry you.' She held the mandolin as if about to play, and next moment I floated up onto the roof. It was night-time and the stars seemed much larger and brighter than in life. I stretched out a hand to touch them, and for a moment held one in my hand. I wanted to put it in a pocket but was still in my bathing suit. A voice said: 'Put it under your chest.' I was trying to fathom out how to do this when I suddenly woke up."

The interpretation: The archetypal nature of this dream is suggested by its most irrational elements: the transformation of the beach into a drawing-room, the dreamer's ability to float to the roof, and his power to touch the stars.

The dreamer has been swimming in the sea, indicating a desire to travel deeper into the archetypal unconscious. However, he then tries to wash the saltwater from his body in a (man-made) shower, suggesting that he wishes to "sanitize" whatever insights he has discovered while swimming there. In this he is only partially successful: too many "other people" (his previous attempts to rationalize the unconscious) are crowding behind him. His back, that aspect of himself that holds him upright in the public world, is "cleaned" but his front, the side visible to his own eyes, is untouched by the sanitizing waters

The sudden transition to the drawing-room, where he drips water onto the carpet, reminds him that he cannot be his true self in an artificial environment, especially under the disapproving gaze of his colleagues, the middle-aged ladies of the dream. The young musician's words are those of the archetypal Anima, telling him that music can "dry" him – in other words that his creative energies can transform the elemental wisdom of the unconscious into the spiritual realm of air.

He then floats up through the house, representing himself, to the roof, where he can see the stars, archetypes of higher states of consciousness, and can seize one with his hands. However, he is still thinking conventionally in wanting to put the star into an outer pocket, and on waking can still not understand how to put it "under his chest", and so integrate his higher self fully into his conscious life.

Dream Symbols

When we wake in the morning, it is often the bizarre nature of our dream memories that convinces us of their unimportance. What possible relevance can the non-sensical images of the night – the faceless stranger, the beast half dog and half horse, the sleek car that turns into a tortoise – have for our conscious life? However, the same question could be asked of a foreign language. Until we learn their meanings, the unfamiliar sounds will make no sense to us; but once we master this new tongue, a whole new dimension of meaning is opened up.

Symbols are the "words" used by dream language: each one represents an idea, a memory, a mood, an insight, arising from the dreamer's unconscious. However, unlike the words of a foreign language, many dream symbols can change their meaning from one participant to another. Moreover, again in contrast to a foreign language, the dream has no fixed grammar, instead linking its semantic units together according to idiosyncratic rules of logic which must be studied carefully before they can be properly teased out and understood.

In every sense, dreaming represents a personal language between the unconscious and the conscious mind, and although we can learn the typical meanings of many dream symbols, we can never be sure that we have understood them – and the connections between them – until we have worked upon them in the light of our unique life-history and our contemporary experience. No matter how weird or laughable particular dream symbols may appear to be, the dream has chosen them for their particular ability to convey the intended message. The most apparently trivial symbol may unlock the most potent memory or the most telling piece of advice.

Generally, Level 1 and 2 dreams, which arise respectively from the preconscious and the personal unconscious (page 23), make most use of symbols that carry particular associations for the dreamer, or that arise from the general currency of everyday life. Many of these have elements of common usage, but others may make sense only to the dreamer. Thus, a tree, for most of us, may represent protection and fertility, but for a dreamer who once fell from a tree's branches as a child it may stand for danger, darkness, and the guilt of a forbidden escapade.

Although making obvious sense, a Level 1 or 2 symbol may carry sufficient emotional charge to be used only in the dreams of particular people. For example, rage may be symbolized for one dreamer by an angry farmer, because it was a farmer who once threatened to shoot him for trespassing; while for another dreamer it may take the form of the Chinese puzzle that once drove her to the limits of frustration over a long summer holiday.

Level 1 and Level 2 symbols can be taken not only from the dreamer's direct experience, but also from more peripheral aspects of life, such as books, plays or TV programmes (even though these may have had little apparent impact on the conscious mind). The dream plunders images shamelessly from the dreamer's memory-banks, choosing the motifs that most readily serve its immediate purposes. We can think of the dream as an mixed-media collage artist, poring with inscutable concentration over a vivid palette, rumaging through boxes of junk and salvaged materials, combining fragments until just the right creative impression has been achieved.

Symbols in Level 3 dreams, by contrast, usually carry a much more universal meaning. Not only are the archetypes common to us all (see pages 34-8) but so are the forms in which they typically arise into awareness. The problem with Level 3 dreams often has less to do with the interpretation of their symbols than with the reluctance of our modern Western consciousness to recognize that dreams can help us contact a reservoir of wisdom frequently beyond the range of our waking minds.

Freud and Jung disagreed fundamentally over what is meant by a symbol, and this was one of the reasons they parted company. Freud assigned a fixed meaning to dream images. For him steeples, guns, knives, doors, caves and the like all represented sexual objects, whenever they appeared in dreams. For Jung, however, this was to treat images as *signs* and not as *symbols*. Jung maintained that the substance of a symbol "consists of our unconscious contents that make themselves felt, yet the conscious is unable to grasp their meaning". A sign, on the other hand, represents a fixed interpretation of a dream image, and therefore one restricted to a meaning that is already conscious. Treating a dream image as a sign not only denies us access to its deeper meaning, but further represses that meaning and thus widens instead of narrowing the gap between the conscious and the unconscious.

For Freud, a phallic symbol represented a penis; for Jung, it was "the creative *mana*, the power of healing and fertility". Most psychologists and anthropologists who have made a study of symbols favour the more creative approach of Jung. The American mythologist Joseph Campell insisted that "consciousness can no more invent, or even predict, an effective symbol than it can foretell or control tonight's dream".

Unlike a sign, a symbol can carry a variety of meanings which, although they are all facets of the same truth, each benefit from separate inspection. Thus, under analysis the image of a gun may emerge even for the same dreamer as representing thunder and lightning, male procreation, destruction, and the toy the dreamer once used to terrify a childhood friend into parting with his candy. Each of these four meanings reflect the central theme of power, but show respectively that power can be used to destroy, to do good, to do evil, or to reinforce a childish urge to intimidate and exploit others.

Perls on Dreams

The American psychiatrist Fritz Perls (1893-1970) is best known as a founder of *gestalt* therapy, which emphasizes the way in which the individual organizes the facts, perceptions and behaviour that make up his or her life, rather than the separate nature of each.

No less than Jung and Freud, Perls stressed the symbolic content of dreams, but he also believed that every character and object in our dreams is a projection of our own self, and of the way in which we have been living our lives. For Perls, dreams represent unfinished emotional business, or "emotional holes", in the dreamer's life history, and their symbolic content stems from the dreamer's personal experience rather than from instinctive or collective drives.

Role play, Perls believed, is a more efficient and accurate technique for interpretation than either free or direct association (see pages 29, 30-31). His method was to ask the dreamer to dramatize each dream image in turn, giving voice even to inanimate dream objects, and sometimes adopting the physical positions that such objects had in the dream, to best represent what message they were trying to convey.

In a dream of a train running through woods, for example, the dreamer may find that the rails, or the trees left behind as the train rushes past, reveal more about his

or her emotional state than does the central image of the train. Act out how the trees feel as they are left behind, Perls might suggest, and what would the rails would say as the train runs over them.

Role play of this kind places interpretation firmly in the dreamer's hands. The therapist may make suggestions, but the dream remains the dreamer's own property: meaning must never be imposed from outside.

There need be no major contradiction between this approach to dreaming and the approaches of Jung and Freud, despite Perls' insistence to the contrary. Both Jung and Freud emphasized that dream images often symbolize aspects of the dreamer's own self, and that in the interpretation of dreams role-play exercises can be a helpful addition to direct or free association. The problem with the Perls method, however, is that the dreamer risks being seduced by his or her acting skills into losing real contact with the dream. Although Perls was confident that he could recognize this effect when it happened, other practitioners of his technique may lack his expert perception. Moreover, as valuable as Perls' methods are for working with dreams at Level 1 and Level 2, they run the risk of undervaluing the shared meaning of dream symbols, and in particular of ignoring the role of the collective unconscious.

Boss on Dreams

The Swiss psychiatrist Medard Boss (b. 1903) posited a relationship between dreaming and existentialism. Existential theory argues that each individual chooses consciously or unconsciously what he or she wishes to be. Thus, for Boss, dreams are not a profound symbolic language, but represent straightforward aspects of existential choice.

The use Boss made of dreams in clinical practice showed clearly that dreams can provide psychological help without being interpreted symbolically. By searching always for symbolic meaning, we run a risk of missing what the dream is actually trying to say. Whereas Freud and Jung concentrated on the deeper Level 2 and 3 dreams, Boss's approach directed attention to the real importance of Level 1 dreams.

In place of association, Boss developed an interpretative method which allowed dreams to tell their own story. This depended less upon theories of the unconscious than upon the ability to see "what is in front of one's face".

In one of his dream experiments, Boss hypnotized five women - three healthy and two neurotic - and suggested that each of them dream of a naked, sexually aroused man known to be in love with them and advancing on them with sexual intent. While the three healthy women followed the given scenario exactly and enjoyably, the dreams of the two neurotic women were anxious and unarousing. In one of them the naked man was replaced by a uniformed soldier armed with a gun with which he nearly shot her. Boss pointed out that there was nothing symbolic about the first three dreams. They were simply open expressions of the dreamers' conscious desires. And even the dream of the soldier had no need of deeper symbolic interpretation: it was a simple reflection of the woman's narrow, fear-drenched world in which men were regarded as threatening.

It would be a mistake to see this existential approach based on Level 1 dreams as negating the existence and importance of Level 2 and Level 3 dreams. In experiments such as this, the dream scenario is placed in the mind by the experimenter, rather than arising from the dreamer's own unconscious. And Jungians and Freudians would point out that the elements that did arise from the unconscious (lover transformed into soldier, penis into gun) could give insights into the *causes* of the woman's neuroses. Associations emerging in response to these images might show, for example, that the dream revealed not only repressed sexuality but also repressed Animus, or that the soldier and the gun represented authoritarian and self-destructive tendencies within the dreamer herself.

The Inner Language

Before Freud and Jung, most scientists argued that dreams were nothing but a random jumble of meaningless images left over from the sensory accumulation of our daily lives. During this century, inspired by Freud's assertion that dreams, in their own way, have meaning, psychologists have proposed numerous, often conflicting, theories to explain the logic they employ.

The often bewildering nature of this logic reflects the dreams' origins outside the tidy confines of the conscious mind. A dream can be a response to events in the outside world, or it can originate within, expressing aspects of the dreamer's deep-seated preoccupations and feelings; it can be a means of fulfilling desires or of highlighting unresolved emotions in the dreamer's everyday life. The contradictions and conflicts implicit in these complex processes are, not unexpectedly, reflected in the grammar and syntax of dreams. Often enigmatic, halting and fragmentary, the language of dreams can warp time, bringing historical and contemporary figures together. It can mix the familiar with the unknown, and work fantastic transformations by its own brand of psychic "magic".

Like certain kinds of movies, the dream world has dissolves in which one scene merges mysteriously into another. Inanimate things move of their own accord, and may talk, and even become intensely threatening. People or animals may fly, or a person may bark like a dog, or walk naked in a crowded place. The meanings dreams hold have to be teased out from such complex and contrary happenings.

The following pages present a "traveller's guide" to the most significant aspects of the dream world, from the logic of dream sequences to the enchanted landscapes that characterize children's dreams and nightmares.

Dream Logic

Until the revolution in dream theory brought about by the work of Freud and Jung, few philosophers disagreed with the nineteenth-century German physicist Theodor Fechner's assertion that in dreams "it is as though psychological activity has been transported from the brain of a reasonable man into that of a fool". His attitude did no more than paraphrase what philosophers had written about dream logic since Roman times, when the statesman and scholar Cicero maintained that "there is no imaginable thing too absurd, too involved, or too abnormal for us to dream about it". The German philosopher Hildebrandt wrote in 1875 of the "laughable contradictions [that the dreamer] is ready to accept in the laws of nature and society", while four years later his compatriot Radestock

asserted that "it seems impossible to detect any fixed laws in this crazy activity … dreams melt into a mad whirl of kaleidoscopic confusion".

What disturbed rational philosophers was not only the apparently "nonsensical" content of the dream images themselves, but also the apparent absence of rational thought and higher mental functions in the logic that links dream images together. In 1877, for example, one writer spoke of "an eclipse of all the logical operations of the mind which are based on relations and connections" so that dreams are in no way "affected by reflection or commonsense".

Freud himself likened a dream, with its absence of helpful interconnections between one image and another, to a sentence that lacks conjunctions – the words such as "and", "if", "because", "when" and "or" that form logical connections between concepts and give language much of its coherence.

However, Freud observed that connections between things can be demonstrated by means other than words – as is the case, for example, with art. He believed that "the madness of dreams may not be without method, and may even be simulated, like that of the Danish prince [Hamlet]". Although dream connections do not follow the rational logic of language and philosophy, it is possible that they adhere to a more oblique rationale in order deliberately to disguise the meaning of the dream.

Clinical experience showed Freud that dream images interconnect by means of four main linking devices. The first is *simultaneity*, when dream images or events are presented together. The second is *contiguity*, when dream images or events are presented in sequence. Thirdly, there is *transformation*, when one image dissolves into another. And lastly, *similarity*, which Freud considered to be the most frequent and important linking device and which operates through association, as one when one object resembles another in some way, or recalls or invokes feelings about that second object. Many of these associations are forgotten or repressed at a conscious level, making the connections harder to unravel, but they can be revealed through appropriate techniques of dream interpretation. By deciphering them, the psychoanalyst lays bare not only the operation of dream logic but also its profound subtlety.

The complex operation of dream logic may be demonstrated by taking a relatively commonplace example: that of dreaming of finding someone's clothes in one's wardrobe. This dream may have a wish-fulfilment aspect, reflecting admiration for the other person's qualities: by acquiring their possessions, we gain some of their characteristics for ourselves. However, there might also be

an aspect of resentment at the intrusion of something foreign into a place that is throroughly private and domestic. This might possibly suggest the envy with which admiration is sometimes tinged. A comparable dream would be the discovery of someone else's clothes on our bed: we might reasonably conclude that this has a similar meaning, except that there is an additional element of inconvenience, in that the clothes are not neatly stowed away but are lying there untidily, requiring us to deal with their presence. Moreover, the bed is an even more intimate place than the wardrobe. Thus, the dream (depending as always on context) might reflect interference by the owner of the clothes in the dreamer's own life.

Dream researchers since Freud have identified *internal consistency* as playing a key role in the operation of dream logic. Analysis of Level 1 and 2 dreams (those generated by the preconscious and personal unconscious) shows that each dreamer may have his or her own particular way of manifesting this consistency.

The most common form which consistency takes, labelled *relative consistency* by the American dream researchers Calvin Hall and Vernon Nordby, lies in the frequency with which various dream images appear to individual dreamers over a period of time. Thus, furniture, body parts, cars and cats may appear in descending order of frequency for one dreamer, while for another subject, women may appear more often than men and outdoor settings more often than indoor. From one year to the next it has been shown that these frequency patterns remain remarkably constant.

Another important form of internal consistency in dreaming is *symbolic consistency*. When using symbols, the dream is unconcerned with how incomprehensible or bizarre they might appear to the conscious mind. It selects them solely on the basis of their associations with the material to be expressed, and repeats the more successful ones in dream after dream to get its message through.

Dream Scenery

A surreal landscape

This desolate piazza scene painted by Giorgio de Chirico captures the elusive weirdness of much dream scenery: the ingredients are not startling in themselves, but the total effect is otherworldly. Apparent incidentals, such as the distant train, may be crucial to the dream's meaning.

Dreams are set most often in familiar locations, reflecting the immediate interests and memories of the dreamer and imbued with all the resonances of his or her social and cultural background. Research has shown the house to be the most common setting; however, as demonstrated by Jung's famous dream which helped to inspire his theory of the Collective Unconscious, the most apparently mundane scenery can carry a remarkable depth of symbolic information.

to examine the dream scenery that featured in their dreams at progressively deeper levels in order to reveal its symbolic meaning. A tree, for example, that initially represents the cherry tree under which the dreamer played as a child, and which therefore stands for shelter and sweetness, can later in the dream serve as a symbol of the mother, later still as the Tree of Life, and finally as the sacrificial tree upon which Christ was crucified. Similarly, a house may be taken progressively to signify the dreamer's body, his

The house that featured in Jung's dream represented his own psyche. Its various floors led progressively deeper into his unconscious until he arrived at the "primitive man" who inhabited the cellar below. On the strength of his own experiences, Jung subsequently encouraged his followers

mind, his mother's body which once nutured and sheltered him, and even – by a common process of dream punning – his father's family or "house". Generally, the more creative and imaginative the dreamer, the more likely it is that such progressive levels of meaning will emerge, and that the dream scenery itself will be varied, colourful and striking.

Many artists have received their inspiration from the scenery of dreams. Painters such as the Italian Surrealist Giorgio de Chirico (1888-1978) and the Belgian Surrealist Paul Delvaux (b. 1897) are particularly credited with capturing the dream atmosphere, drawing also upon Freudian dream symbolism and setting familiar images in bizarre contexts. It is the juxtaposition of the ordinary and the extraordinary, captured in their paintings, that gives dream scenery its special quality, and that invests nightmares with their chilling power. A house may be the dreamer's own, yet in the juxtaposed horror of the nightmare it is saturated with an eerie emptiness never experienced in waking life.

As with the more obvious, foreground elements in a dream, an item of dream scenery can suddenly transform itself. A carpet may turn into a swamp, a distant farm may turn into a slaughter-house. By means of these reversals, the nightmare drives its message home, startling the mind out of conventional habits of thinking so that deep emotions and anxieties are hauntingly exposed.

Dream landscapes, far from being merely background, are often deeply experienced, rather than merely observed. A landscape may ache with loneliness, or be suffused with a mysterious sense of well-being. If the landscape has gentle contours and evokes strong feelings, one possible interpretation is that it symbolizes the body, especially the mother's body. Freud believed that landscapes in dreams, especially those containing rocky crags (male) or wooded hills (female), often operate as symbols of genitalia. Dream places can also represent the topography of the mind itself: for example, a strange neighbourhood in a remote part of town, can be a symbol of the unconscious. Nocturnal scenes, similarly, can suggest the murky depths of the inner self.

It is vital, during interpretation, to remember the details of the dream landscape if the full meaning of the dream is to be revealed. If a scene is set in a garden, is it formal or informal in design? well-kept or overgrown? If there is a road, does it wind and double back upon itself, or is it long and straight, an easy journey home?

Even those parts of the scenery that appear to be merely backdrops can have a significance which may emerge as central when analyzed by techniques such as those of Fritz Perls, including dramatic enactment by the dreamer of each remembered aspect of the dream (see page 42).

Because any element in the scenery can also represent a different person or a different aspect of the dreamer's personality, it is important to establish if possible what relationship each element has to the dreamer. Does the dreamer own the setting, or does it have associations, however strange, with someone of his or her acquaintance? What emotion does the scenery arouse? If it could speak, what would it say? If green fields in a dream are bordered by a distant town, does this make the dreamer feel secure to see evidence of civilization near by, or does it provoke resentment at the man-made intrusion?

Dream scenery is the landscape of the imagination, a glimpse of the dreamer's total imaginative fabric into which are woven all his life-memories and emotions, wishes and fears. It is both the setting and the content of a dream. It works at one and the same time to give dreams their enchanted quality and to convey or support their deeper levels of meaning.

The more closely we attend to dreams, the more vivid and impressive dream scenery becomes, and the more powerful a vehicle of dream consciousness. Salvador Dali strove not only to remember the finest details of his dream landscapes but actually to induce them. He is said to have enjoyed dozing in a chair, his chin in his hands and his elbow supported upon a table, so that every time he fell asleep his chin dropped and he awoke from a hypnogogic dream full of the surreal, enchanted scenery which figured so prominently in his paintings.

CASE FILE IV

The dreamer is a male sales executive working for a large conglomerate. He has always wanted to be a novelist, but now spends much of his time writing misleading but highly effective publicity material.

The dream: "I was in a hairdressers' awaiting my turn. The salon was small and dark, and I had the impression of brown paintwork and a rather seedy atmosphere. There were two men ahead of me, sitting on my right, with their heads in their newspapers, but the hairdresser called me first. It seemed that he knew me, and that I had been there before.

"I was rather put out by this, and thought that he wanted to ingratiate himself with me. When I went to sit in the chair, however, I found that I was in the salon on my own. The mirror in front of me was old and the silvering had decayed with the damp, so that I was unable to see myself reflected in it. Then I was outside, looking into the windows of some stores. I think that I was trying to find some scissors to cut my own hair, but was unsuccessful. I heard a hissing sound and said to myself: 'the balloon has burst'."

The interpretation: The dreamer associated hair and his dream trip to the hairdresser with "a rather seedy" and ineffectual vanity, and associated the hairdresser's ingratiating behaviour with the way in which others lavish praise and attention where it is not due, a situation that he clearly associated with his work as a copy writer for a large advertising company.

The two silent men should have been called to the barber's chair before him. Yet they had their heads buried in newspapers, indicating that in spite of the dreamer's success in business, there are deeper, still mute and latent aspects of his self, such as his gifts as a writer, which should be given priority.

The absence of the hairdresser when the dreamer found himself in the chair suggested that taking credit where it was not due would be of no benefit to him in the long run, and would prove to have won him false friends.

The dreamer felt that the mirror in which he could not see his face was a reminder not so much of a loss of identity as of a lack of self-knowledge. He had allowed his ability to know himself to decay in the environment of falsity and deception in which he found himself currently passing his professional life.

This theme is emphasized further by the sterile earthiness, or materiality, of the brown paintwork in the early part of the dream

The hairdressers' salon, as well as the dreamer's subsequent attempt to find what he was seeking in store windows, indicated that the dreamer was trying to satisfy his needs by looking for opportunities outside himself. The hunt for scissors suggested, however, his recognition of the need to limit his vanity. The themes of self-knowledge and the deflation of vanity appear to be taken up again in the final image, with the sound of escaping air and dreamer's own remark that "the balloon has burst".

CASE FILE V

*The dreamer is a woman in her late twenties, who holds a
responsible and challenging executive position with a firm of real estate
agents in a big city.*

The dream: "This is one of a series of dreams in which I find myself surrounded by old and broken objects, or new gadgets that, whatever I do, somehow refuse to work.

"In this dream, I found myself standing at the top of a long flight of steps. They seemed to lead down to a backyard full of rubble and scrap metal, yet the steps themselves were wide and grand, like those in the garden of a chateau.

"I could see a man in the scrap yard working on an old car, and I asked him why it wouldn't go. He said it worked now, because he had fixed it, and then we were driving down a freeway, but going so fast that I felt afraid the car would fall to pieces. I asked him to stop and he seemed to slow down, but when I looked out of the window, I could only see a blur of speed."

The interpretation: Steps downward usually represent a way into the personal unconscious. The dreamer claims to enjoy her dreams, and has high expectations of what they may reveal to her (the grand stairway), yet in fact the steps lead only to the broken, discarded rubbish of old memories and useless objects.

But things aren't exactly as they seem. There is a man working among the junk in the backyard, signifying that psychological healing and creative activity continue in the unconscious mind, even though we are usually unaware of them, and that what may seem like psychic rubbish can be of great value, if we approach it in the proper way.

He tells her that he has "fixed" the old car, a means of travelling, of getting somewhere, and perhaps in this case symbolic of a disappointed aspiration or ambition of the the dreamer's earlier life.

They speed away together along a highway that represents escape from the confines of the city (other people), but the car is outside the dreamer's control, and she is afraid, though more for the safety of the car than for herself. The ideas or ambitions which the car represents are perhaps re-emerging (or are likely to re-emerge) into consciousness in too hasty a form for their own or for her own good.

The dreamer wants to slow down, but even after the car appears to have done so, the scenery outside is still a blur. She is travelling too fast to recognize or hold onto personal landmarks and re-orientate herself in a new world. The car does not fall apart, however, and her driver travels the freeway without disaster.

The dreamer confesses that she has been worried that her dream world seems to bear little relation to her waking life, and considers that her dream is telling her that she must act with more trust and courage in her attempts to journey into the world of the unconscious. If she does so, the now blurred landmarks of her inner life may become clearer to her.

Children's Dreams

We are born dreamers. We may even dream in the womb and certainly spend much of our early life in dreams. About 60 per cent of the sleep of newborn babies is passed in the REM (rapid eye movement) state (see page 14) where most dreaming occurs, three times the amount spent by most adults. Since babies sleep for fourteen or more hours a day, this adds up to a great deal of dream time.

Although it is obviously impossible for us to know exactly what small babies' dreams contain, it is probable that much of their dream content is triggered by physical sensations, or consists of dreams about physical sensations. After the first month of their lives, visual and auditory images probably also begin to play a part.

Once children are old enough to tell us about their dreams, the content primarily reflects their waking interests and emotions.

Robert Van de Castle and Donna Kramer of the University of Virginia analyzed many hundreds of dreams from children aged between two and twelve, and found that from an early age girls' dreams were longer than those of boys, and contained more people and references to clothes, while boys dreamed more about implements and objects. Animals featured much more prominently in children's dreams than in those of adults, and the ratio of frightening animals such as lions, gorillas, alligators and wolves to non-frightening animals such as sheep, butterflies and birds was far higher.

This frequency of animal images would seem to reflect children's basic interests, and the way in which animals symbolize their wishes and fears. Van de Castle, however, considers that these themes may also rise from the more primitive, animistic nature of their thinking.

Children report around twice as many aggressive acts in their dreams as do adults. Occasionally, children play the role of aggressors, but more usually they are victims, and fear has thus been shown to be their most common dream emotion.

Robert Kegan, an American developmental psychologist, has suggested that this high level of aggressive acts represents the difficulty that young children have in integrating their own powerful, spontaneous impulses into the social order and control demanded of them by adults. The wild animals, monsters and bogey men of children's dreams also seem to symbolize children's inner awareness that such impulses lurk just below the conscious surface of their behaviour and may break out and wreak havoc in the conscious mind if self-control is relaxed.

For Kegan, the common experience in children's dreams of being eaten alive is particularly significant, since it represents a terror of losing an emerging yet fragile sense of self in the face of powerful conflicts between inner impulses and outer demands.

In psychoanalytical theory, as well as representing aspects of the dreamer's self, the bogeymen of children's dreams can also symbolize parents and other powerful adults. A young child has serious problems in consciously reconciling the loving, providing aspects of a mother or father with their function as agents of discipline and fear. Dream witches and wolves are thus ways of representing and accepting the punitive role that parents play, while the child's own acts of aggression toward parental symbols in dreams can symbolize rivalry directed toward the same-sex parent, or simply their wish to be free of the dominating force that adults exercise in daily life.

Freud laid particular emphasis upon this last, wish-fulfilling, aspect of children's dreaming, so much so in fact that he considered that children's dreams "raise no problems for solution", and are "quite uninteresting compared to the dreams of adults".

He believed that a child's relative lack of sexual desire during the so-called "latency" period (approximately age seven to puberty) simplifies the nature of their wish-fulfilment during this time, leaving the way clear for "the other of the two great vital instincts" to assert itself – namely, the desire for food.

Jungian psychology, however, claims a level of interpretation for children's dreams that goes beyond that of wishes and desires, recognizing in the bogeyman, hero and heroine the archetypal images already activated in the child's unconscious, and symbolizing not only aspects of waking life but also the child's mystical sense of his or her own inner nature.

Anthropologists have identified several cultures in which childhood dreaming is allowed by society to play a far stronger role in children's psychological development. While researching among the Temiar people of Indonesia, Richard Noone and Kilton Stewart discovered that children were routinely asked to recount their dreams each morning so that the adults of the group could "train" them to deal with their dream fears and challenges in order to enhance their psychological development actually during sleep.

Joan Halifax, among several anthropologists interested in tribal attitudes to dreams, has emphasized the crucially important part that dreams play, sometimes from as early as five years old, in the life and training of the shaman, and in helping him or her to travel in and deal with the spirit world.

So strong is the belief in the creative power of dreaming among Australian shamanic cultures that children are taught that the world itself was brought into being during the "Dreamtime".

However the images, events and symbols of childhood dreams are understood, there is little doubt that these dreams play a vital role in the psychological development of children, and that they can have a powerful influence upon what happens in the years to come.

CASE FILE VI

*The dreamer is an eight-year-old girl who is having problems with her teacher
at school. This dream took place after a school trip to a science museum,
which the teacher claims the child did not enjoy.*

The dream: "There was a big truck with a boiler thing behind it outside the school, and my teacher said she thought it was going to explode.

"A man got out of the truck and came toward me, and I was frightened and ran away. Then I was in the car with my Daddy, and we were driving away from this man, and my Daddy went through a red stop light and up on the pavement, but there was nobody there. Then someone came up to us and said that the thing had exploded, and my Daddy said we must go back to the school and see what it was that had happened. But I didn't want to go back there."

The interpretation: Children's dreams tend to be more episodic and fragmented than those of adults. This reflects their more limited experience, but may also be caused by memory failure or a tendency to run several dreams into one. It is a mistake to impose an outside, adult interpretation on children's dreams; instead, children must be helped to find their own associations to their dreams so that they can interpret them themselves and draw their own conclusions.

This girl has been having problems with her teacher, and although her parents have been questioning her, she is unable to communicate her exact feelings about her troubles. In the dream, the threatened explosion outside the school is clearly associated with the teacher ("my teacher said … "), and may represent what appears to the child as the teacher's unpredictable outbursts of anger. The image of a boiler to symbolize anger may emerge from an unsatisfactory visit to the science museum, and may also originate from the cliché "to boil over with rage". The threatening man who looms toward her from the truck may symbolize the fear she has of her teacher, and her wish to escape from her.

She relies on her father to make good her escape ("then I was in the car with my Daddy"), but knows that he can only do so by breaking what she knows full well are the rules of the adult world, jumping a red stop light as they drive away from school. But his efforts come to nothing; breaking the rules gets them nowhere: "there was nobody there" when the car mounted the pavement. As soon as he hears of the teacher's anger ("someone said that the thing had exploded") he decides that they must return to school, the scene of the child's problems. Although she "didn't want to go", she is unable to do anything about it on her own, and realizes that she must learn to accept the sometimes unpredictable and frightening aspects of the adult world that her teacher both embodies and symbolizes.

CASE FILE VII

The dreamer is a female athlete noted for her single-minded determination on the track, but whose relationships and wider social life have always been troubled and unsatisfactory.

The dream: "It was summer and I was standing on an open road stretching into the distance. I could feel the hot sun on the back of my neck. Then I saw someone approaching in the distance, and realized at once that though they were running they were moving in terrifying slow-motion. It was as if I could see them coming toward me and at the same time see them in profile. I was rooted to the spot and everything went deathly cold. Then somehow I was sitting on the back of a horse, but it just kept eating the grass, and refused to move. I dug my heels in, but they just sank into its sides and some horrible stuff came out. Then I was suddenly off the horse and chasing someone, determined to catch them and teach them a lesson for giving me these nightmares. I don't know if it was a man or a woman, but I rang along a huge tall corridor, with very high dusty windows. The creature ran into a room at the end of the corridor, and I thought, 'Now I've got you'; but when I ran into the room the door slammed and locked behind me, and the creature turned a horrible face toward me and screamed in triumph. When I woke sweating and shaking, I could still feel its fingers around my neck."

The interpretation: The dreamer reports this as one of the vivid and strangely "real" nightmares, laden with anxiety, that have plagued her since childhood. They typically start with a man or woman running in deliberate and menacing slow motion. This image often throws her into a state of shock, from which she has to struggle to free herself if she is not to be a passive victim of whatever horror is to follow.

As an athlete, the dreamer can usually "solve" her problems by running faster than her opponents, but in her anxiety dream nothing allows her to escape, even though the "someone" who menacingly approaches her is moving deliberately slowly.

She herself interpreted this as representing her deeply felt powerlessness when dealing with other people, a powerlessness whose causes she must try hard to identify.

The horse may represent the natural force of her emotions, which is unable to take her along the stretch of open road toward a stable relationship. Only "horrible stuff" emerges from the seat of her emotions.

The tall corridor along which she pursues the cause of her problems stands as a symbol for the single-mindedness with which she approaches life, and which prevents her from seeing out of the dusty windows in order to get a broader view.

She interpreted the terrible final scene, trapped in a locked room and faced by the "horrible" demon of her own anxiety, in these words: "It means I lead myself into my own difficulties; I am my own worst enemy."

Dream Directory

Dreams are a conversation we have with ourselves, in a symbolic language that sends messages between the unconscious and conscious levels of our minds. We are the authors and actors of our dreams, and ultimately the best judges of their meanings. No dream interpretation offered by an outsider is likely to be correct unless the dreamer recognizes it as authentic.

In Level 1 and 2 dreams (see page 23), which arise from the personal unconscious, the dreaming mind communicates through the use of symbols that carry particular associations for the dreamer, mostly originating in recent waking events. Many dream directories attempt a definitive interpretation of such dreams, but such prescriptive equivalences are avoided here. This directory is intended as a starting point to stimulate interpretation, so that we can understand the wealth of imagery available to the dreaming mind.

Level 3 dreams, from the collective unconscious (page 23), find their associations in a wider pool of archetypes (page 34). These appear in our dreams as the gods, heroes, demons and damsels we know from our legends and myths. Jung developed a technique known as amplification (page 31) to tease these meanings from the imagination.

The first part of this Directory looks from cause to effect: it is organized according to underlying Themes, analyzing some common ways in which our waking preoccupations are represented. The second part looks from effect to cause: it examines common dream phenomena and offers possible explanations for them.

The dreaming mind is adept at selecting whatever material best helps to convey its intended meaning. After studying the Directory, you may even find that your dreams begin to use these themes and images as a language that your conscious mind can understand.

Part I: Themes

Contents

Change and Transition

Our conscious minds are often unaware of the psychological and emotional upheavals that follow major changes in our lives. However, the un-conscious tends to know better, and some psychologists now believe that in the two years following even propitious events such as marriage or promotion we are more prone not only to psychological disturbance but also to physical ailments that may appear as symptoms of unrest.

If in our unconscious minds we are nervous and insecure in the face of change, our dreams may be filled with comforting images of our former ways of life and most familiar surroundings. The dreaming mind may also show its anxiety about a particular transition by an exaggerated sense of strangeness, perhaps imbued with feelings of dread.

Change is the only constant, however, and more usually our dreams advise us of the desirability and inevitability of change. They may indicate which directions we should take, warning us of potential pitfalls, or providing guidance and encouragement during the period of transition.

The need for change may appear in dreams as an attempt to exchange old or faulty goods in a store, or as the act of redecorating our homes, changing our clothes, or buying new books or CDs to replace the ones that we had bought before. Dreams of crossing a road, river or bridge may indicate the risks that changes may bring, or symbolize its irrevocable nature.

The Jungian technique of amplification (see page 31) may reveal associations with mythical images of transition, such as the Greek hero Herakles crossing the River Styx: on one side lies the land of the living; on the other side, death, the entrance to the Underworld. Jonah's sea crossing, shipwreck and journey inside the whale across stormy seas carries similarly archetypal imagery, suggesting the dangerous crossing of a threshold, the past left behind and the future stretching mysteriously ahead.

Object coming to life
If an inanimate object comes to life in a dream, it may be that a previously unacknowledged inner potential is now ripe for development. If the metamorphosis is frightening, such inner energies may need acknowledging and channelling into more acceptable forms.

Transformations

A change during a dream from autumn and winter through to spring and summer may indicate deep inner transformations within the dreamer. Movement in the opposite direction may suggest the need for a fallow, recuperative period or for more communication with the dark world of the unconscious. The transition from day to night may carry a similar message. A bridge in a dream can be a classic symbol of change, spanning the boundary between the past and future, suggesting the opportunities that may be available on the other side.

Unfamiliar surroundings

If unfamiliar surroundings make the dreamer feel lost, apprehensive, or full of regret, the dreaming mind may be trying to say that he or she is not yet ready to leave an old way of life behind: it is too soon to master a new set of circumstances. On the other hand, feelings of excitement accompanying the dream suggest that the dreamer is ready for change, and should seize whatever opportunity has arisen. To dream of finding ourselves in unfamiliar or restrictive clothing often represents an anxiety about being placed in a new and unaccustomed role.

Direction and Identity

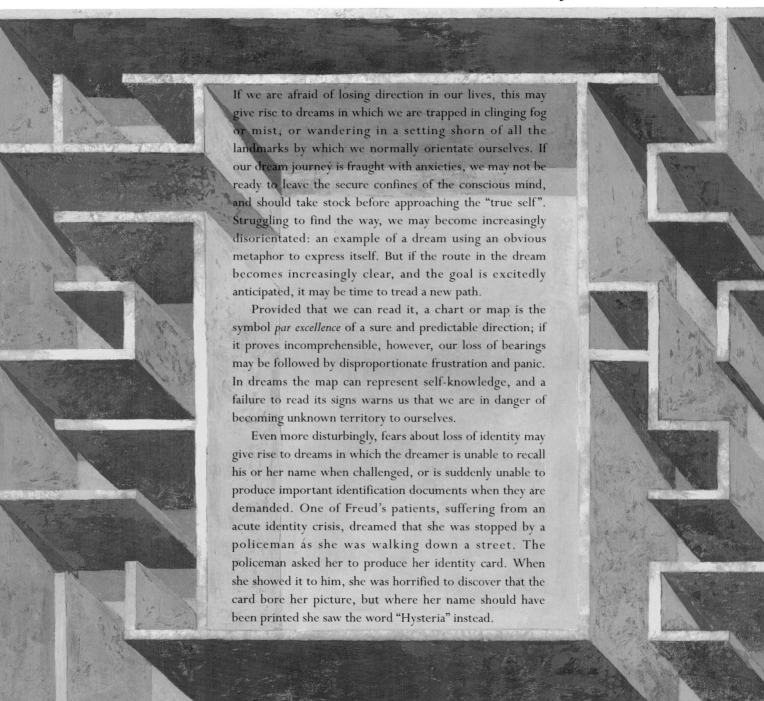

If we are afraid of losing direction in our lives, this may give rise to dreams in which we are trapped in clinging fog or mist, or wandering in a setting shorn of all the landmarks by which we normally orientate ourselves. If our dream journey is fraught with anxieties, we may not be ready to leave the secure confines of the conscious mind, and should take stock before approaching the "true self". Struggling to find the way, we may become increasingly disorientated: an example of a dream using an obvious metaphor to express itself. But if the route in the dream becomes increasingly clear, and the goal is excitedly anticipated, it may be time to tread a new path.

Provided that we can read it, a chart or map is the symbol *par excellence* of a sure and predictable direction; if it proves incomprehensible, however, our loss of bearings may be followed by disproportionate frustration and panic. In dreams the map can represent self-knowledge, and a failure to read its signs warns us that we are in danger of becoming unknown territory to ourselves.

Even more disturbingly, fears about loss of identity may give rise to dreams in which the dreamer is unable to recall his or her name when challenged, or is suddenly unable to produce important identification documents when they are demanded. One of Freud's patients, suffering from an acute identity crisis, dreamed that she was stopped by a policeman as she was walking down a street. The policeman asked her to produce her identity card. When she showed it to him, she was horrified to discover that the card bore her picture, but where her name should have been printed she saw the word "Hysteria" instead.

Mazes

A maze in a dream usually relates to the dreamer's descent into the unconscious. It may represent the complex defences put up by the conscious ego to prevent unconscious wishes and desires from emerging into the light.

Car losing control

Anxiety about a loss of direction in life may cause dreams of hurtling out of control in a car or train. Similarly, fears of loss of personal identity can prompt dream experiences in which the dreamer hunts desperately for the correct road or street in a strange town.

Masks

These represent the way that we present ourselves to the outside world and even to ourselves. If the dreamer is unable to remove a mask, or is forced by others to wear one, this suggests that the real self is becoming increasingly obscured.

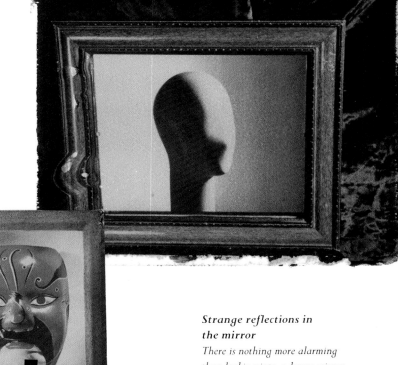

Strange reflections in the mirror

There is nothing more alarming than looking into a dream mirror and seeing someone else's face reflected there. This is the classic dream to represent identity crisis, the sudden sense of not knowing who we are. The face in the mirror may give clues as to the nature of the identity problem. Closed eyes often indicate an unwillingness to face reality.

Success and Failure

How we react to success and failure does much to dictate the future course of our lives. These two sides of the same coin are among the most common preoccupations of our dreams, as of our waking lives. Whatever our anxieties, we often believe in our hearts that failure can be overcome; more certain still is the knowledge that success is usually short-lived. When warring against the Greeks, the Persian prince Xerxes dreamed of a crown of olives whose branches spread out over the world but then suddenly vanished, an accurate omen that his conquests would soon be lost.

Many other monarchs, generals and statesmen have had prophetic dreams of success or failure. King Richard III of England dreamed of evil spirits before his defeat at the Battle of Bosworth. On the night before Waterloo, Napoleon dreamed of a procession of figures bearing symbols of his triumphs, which were ominously followed by a figure in chains and fetters. Otto von Bismarck, prime minister of Prussia, dreamed of his country's rise to power before it grew to become the lynchpin of a new unified Germany. However, most dreams of success or failure are linked less to actual events than to the dreamer's state of mind.

Prizes

Trophies carry a value far beyond their material worth – just as a cup's value is not intrinsic, but depends upon what it can hold. In dreams, even if the nature of the prize remains obscure, the sense of triumph is normally unmistakable.

Dreams of failure often contain situations such as ringing a doorbell or knocking on a door without reply, or finding oneself without money to pay for a taxi or settle a debt, or losing a contest or an argument. Success in dreams may be indicated by a favourable outcome to a transaction, often accompanied by feelings of fulfilment or even elation. A fence or hurdle commonly stands for a particular challenge confronting the dreamer in waking life. Jumping over the obstacle may represent not only the possibility of success but also the confidence upon which that success may depend, and which the dreamer must strive to acquire. Level 3 dreams (see page 23) sometimes reflect success at a deep level of personal growth and transformation.

Amplification of Level 3 dreams may reveal associations with classical themes, such as the story of the Greek warrior Bellerophon who captured the winged horse Pegasus and soared toward Mount Olympus in an attempt to claim a place among the gods. However, Pegasus threw him; and having fallen back to earth the warrior passed the rest of his days as an outcast on the Plain of Wandering. Such archetypes remind us of the dangers of overstretching our natural limits.

Communication breakdown

Failure to make oneself heard, or otherwise to give a good account of oneself, strongly suggests feelings of inadequacy. By drawing these feelings to the attention of the dreamer, the dream indicates the need to confront them in waking life. Failure to make oneself understood on the telephone can suggest weaknesses in the dreamer's ideas or in the ability to convey them convincingly to others.

Winning a race

This indicates a recognition of the potential within ourselves. To come second or third may suggest aspirations beyond one's abilities.

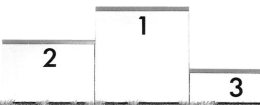

Anxiety

Anxiety is probably the most common emotional state expressed in our dreams. In waking life, the mind is often able to distract itself from troublesome issues, but in sleep they rise into awareness, filling our dreams with unsettling, highly charged symbols, and with dark, troubled moods. Such dreams not only indicate how deeply rooted our anxieties can be, but also they remind us of the need to tackle the source of these worries, either by confronting a specific external challenge or by learning to be less fearful of life's predicaments.

Anxiety dreams are recognizable by the emotional charge that they carry. Typically, the dreamer has the sensation of trying to cope with several duties simultaneously, or of trying to complete a never-ending task. Other anxiety dreams include walking through clinging mud, moving in agonizingly slow motion, and crawling through a narrow tunnel (a symbol often believed to represent birth anxiety), being choked by smoke, watching helplessly as cherished possessions are destroyed, and trying in a high wind to hold together the broken fragments of something the dreamer holds dear. If anxiety stems from social inadequacy, the dream may involve public embarrassment such as spilling a drink, grotesque incompetence on a crowded dance floor, or forgetting the names of important guests while trying to introduce them.

The dreaming mind is not always shy of melodrama – a walk to the scaffold, or falling into the hands of evil captors, or being forced into committing some terrible crime, may reflect relatively mundane problems. The point of such extreme forms of terror is to impress upon the subject the need to bring into consciousness (as a prelude to dealing with them) repressed desires and energies of a powerful nature.

Whatever form they take, anxiety dreams are not there to torment the dreamer, but to draw attention to the urgency of identifying and dealing with the sources of anxiety, which may wreak havoc in the unconscious if left to themselves.

Falling

Anxiety dreams often place us in overwhelming situations in which we are powerless to act. Among the most common is the dream of falling from a great height, an image that emphasizes that the dreamer has climbed too high in personal or professional life and may now be ready for a fall.

Drowning

Dreams of drowning, or struggling in deep water, may represent the dreamer's fear of being engulfed by forces hidden in the deepest reaches of our unconscious minds. Such dreams often indicate that control over the unconscious needs to be relaxed slowly.

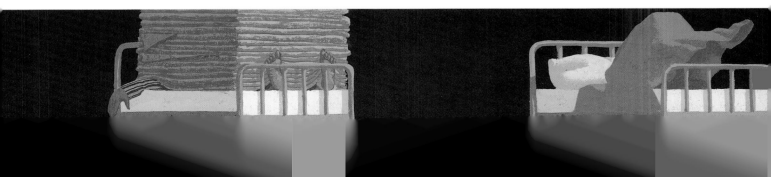

Frustrations

Being arrested often indicates feelings of guilt, especially if stolen goods or past misdemeanours are subsequently discovered. To dream of failing to obtain what we want often suggests a lack of communication between the conscious and unconscious minds, indicating that unconscious instincts and desires have been repressed by the ego and are unable to satisfy themselves in waking life. Dreams of being trapped may also indicate that desires or creative energies have been repressed and must be revealed before they damage the conscious mind.

Being chased

Dreams of being chased by an unseen but terrifying presence usually indicate that aspects of the self are clamouring for integration into consciousness. The dreamer's fear usually dissipates if he or she can turn and face the pursuer, and gain clues as to what this symbol represents at the conscious level. The Senoi people of Malaysia consider that the very act of facing fears in one's dreams increases courage in waking life.

Trying to run

One of the most common anxiety dreams involves trying to run but finding that one's legs stay rooted to the spot. Similar are dreams of walking through clinging mud, or moving in painfully slow motion. Recent research suggests that such dreams may result from mechanisms in the brain that prevent us from acting out our dreams as we sleep, stopping us from running in our beds or wreaking havoc in the bedroom.

Well-being and Optimism

An optimistic or happy dream can occur at any time, even when when we are feeling the full weight of life's burdens. Such dreams may leave us exalted and content not only with our everyday lives but also with the world as a whole. They may introduce us to higher beings, or take us flying through the dream world, opening our minds to the infinity of time and space.

Sometimes optimistic dreams contain symbols of good luck or peace – either images that are personal to the dreamer such as a lucky stone or colour, or cultural symbols of good fortune such as black cats, four-leafed clovers, doves or olive branches. Some people interpret these dreams as prophetic of future success; others believe that they show that the journey toward fulfilment has begun, but without any guarantee that the goal will be reached.

Dreams that present configurations of the dreamer's lucky number are usually a cause for optimism. More potent still are dream visions of the rainbow, the archetypal symbol of hope and reconciliation. The dreamer may seem to be watching a rainbow forming in the sky over his or her house (a symbol of the self), or flooding the far-off hills in light (a symbol of achievement). In Level 3 dreams (see page 23) the dreamer may even be bathed in rainbow light, suggesting a baptism into a new phase of personal growth and development.

Honey and bees
The Israelites believed that the Promised Land flowed with milk and honey; the Greeks and Romans regarded honey as the food of the gods. Bees were endowed with special wisdom, and their appearance in dreams was regarded as an auspicious symbol, predicting peace and prosperity.

As in waking life, colours in dreams can represent individual emotional or spiritual states. Blue, for example, is often thought to symbolize melancholia, but it may also stand for the deep contemplative waters of the unconscious mind; while red represents not only anger, but also (depending on context) the passion and drive of fire.

Lucid dreams (see page 46), generally characterized by feelings of joy and excitement, often contain particularly vivid and stimulating colours that transform the dream landscape into a world of magical and startling beauty.

When worked on through the technique of amplification, dreams that indicate well-being and optimism may produce associations with the Elysian fields, the paradise of classical mythology. Christian symbolism is filled with accounts of paradisal Golden Ages, from the Garden of Eden to the New Jerusalem of Revelations, an era of spiritual well-being that will last a thousand years.

The gate is an enduring symbol in dreams of an entry into a new world of opportunity and enlightenment. Gates that open invitingly before a dreamer may confirm the possibility of initiation onto a higher plane of self-knowledge. Even a gate that appears closed may suggest that the dreamer is now ready to attempt the next stage of his or her inner journey.

Light

For Jung, the appearance of light in dreams "always refers to consciousness". Such dreams confirm that profound insights are illuminating or about to illuminate the conscious mind of the dreamer, as if he or she is about to "see the light". Through amplification of these dreams, the dreamer may find religious associations, for example with Christ as the light of the world or with the Boddhisattva Amitabha, the Buddhist deity of "boundless light", the essence from which all creation arises.

Colours

Bright or vivid colours often indicate the onset of a "grand dream" (see page 30), involving archetypal symbols and themes. Orange is often used as a symbol of hope and well-being.

Authority and Responsibility

People in positions of authority and responsibility in waking life often report dreams that reflect their status. Such dreams may involve episodes such as dealing with emergencies, sitting at a desk and receiving requests for decisions from all sides, or carrying symbols of office such as a ceremonial chain.

On occasions, authority and responsibility dreams merge into anxiety dreams. The dreamer may seem to be giving orders which no-one obeys, or suffering a sudden rejection at the ballot box, or at the hands of superiors. Such images draw attention to the dreamer's feelings of insecurity, and indicate the need to become more fully integrated into his or her public role. Authority and

Wearing a tall hat
Crowns and tall hats are traditional symbols of authority, raising the wearer above his or her peers and colleagues. To dream of having a crown or tall hat knocked off one's head may symbolize anxieties about the loss or inappropriateness of the dreamer's status.

Stacks of paper
To dream of a desk stacked high with an unending pile of papers is a typical anxiety dream for those in authority, suggesting the near-impossibility of handling the growing demands and stress that come with increasing responsibility. The dream may help the dreamer to see that he or she is not dealing effectively enough with incoming work.

responsibility dreams may also reveal frustrations and resentments felt about the over-dependency of other people: such dreams fulfil a dual purpose by allowing these feelings harmless expression and by drawing attention to the over-stretched role that the dreamer is being called upon to play in waking life.

Many people dream of sitting at the head of a long table. The longer the table, the more people the individual at the head has under his or her command. If there is insufficient food to go around it may indicate a failure to provide nourishment for dependants, while rejection of the food by those sitting at the table suggests disagreement with the dreamer or a refusal to accept his or her authority.

When amplified, authority and responsibility dreams can reveal classical links: for example, associations with the account in the *Aeneid* of the Roman hero Aeneas. While fleeing from the flames of burning Troy, Aeneas bravely fulfilled his responsibilities to his family by leading his father and son to safety. This was not an easy task since he had to carry his father, the aged Anchises, on his back while leading Ascanius, his young son, by the hand.

Such classical archetypes may remind the dreamer of the psychological importance and intrinsic heroism of facing up to one's duties and responsibilities in waking life, and of wielding the power of one's own authority for the good of others.

Relationships

When analyzing dream relationships, it is particularly important to remember that the dreaming mind is intent not upon duplicating reality but, rather, upon commenting on reality. It thus frequently uses dream characters as symbols rather than as attempts at depicting actual people with whom the dreamer is involved in waking life.

As revealed by direct association, a complete stranger in a dream may represent characteristics of a wife or husband, while a partner may stand for some aspect of the dreamer. The dream is therefore more concerned with its message than with portraying people as they really are. The dreamer is already familiar with waking appearances, and the task of the dreaming mind is to draw attention to those things that are less obvious or that have been left unacknowledged.

Thus, in the course of dream analysis, a friend transformed into a stranger may reveal a fundamental ambivalence in the dreamer's general feelings about friendship. Sudden rejection of a loved one may indicate the dreamer's rejection of some part of his or her own nature. Separation from one's children may suggest the loss of cherished ideals or the failure of personal ambitions.

At other times, dream characters do indeed seem to represent themselves, but do so in order to draw attention to unrecognized aspects of our relationships with them.

Mending things

Repairing an appliance such as a radio or refrigerator often indicates the need to work at a relationship to prevent it from deteriorating. An appliance that has been unaccountably dismantled may also carry this meaning.

Frequent dreams of family members may show an over-dependence upon the family, whether in the form of over-protection or perhaps an inability to break free from family ties. New parents often dream of accidently rolling upon a baby in the bed, and are probably expressing in dream symbolism their anxiety about their new nuturing role.

Even inanimate objects may represent relationships in our dreams. One of Freud's patients once dreamed of borrowing a comb, and this was interpreted as revealing her anxiety about a mixed marriage.

Failure to make a telephone connection may suggest loss of intimacy in a relationship, while dreams of intense heat or cold may reflect burning passion or cool indifference toward a partner.

During amplification, symbols from a Level 3 dream may provide associations with mythical themes such as the love between the Egyptian deities Isis and Osiris. Isis, the ancient Egyptian symbol of motherhood, is said to have loved Osiris even in the womb. No less strong was the love of Orpheus for Eurydice. Orpheus was a minstrel, linked with the gods Dionysos and Apollo; his music tamed wild animals, rivers and storms and even persuaded the rulers of the dead to let him take his lover Eurydice back from the realm of death. He was told that he could lead her away if he did not look back while leaving the Underworld, but his

Birds

Animals frequently symbolize aspects of relationships, and each dream animal usually embodies the emotion with which its behaviour is linked. Territorial birds such as blackbirds can represent jealousy, while thieving birds such as magpies may suggest a threat to a relationship from an outside party, or aspects of the self stolen by a friend or partner.

Hotel

In dreams, hotels often represent impermanence, a point of transition in a relationship, or a shift or even a loss of personal identity. They may also suggest the price that has to be paid to sustain a relationship.

Feathers

Feathers, whether or not they appear in the same dream as birds, often represent a gift, expressing the desire to show warmth or tenderness to someone close to the dreamer.

Fire

This is a powerful and ambivalent dream symbol. Fire destroys, but it also cleanses and purifies. In dreams it can signal a new beginning, or represent disruptive emotions – perhaps the flames of passion or envy.

love for her was too great and when he turned around to see her, he lost her for eternity. Even after being killed and torn apart by the maenads for refusing any longer to honour Dionysos, his head continued to sing, lamenting the passing of his love.

Another archetype sometimes revealed through amplification is the witch, symbol of the all-consuming, punitive, terrifying role of the Great Mother, and established throughout the world in myths and fairy tales. For example, in the story of Hanzel and Gretel the witch is an evil old woman who attempts to eat the two young children who innocently chance upon her cottage buried deep inside the forest.

Rather as the witch can symbolize the destructive aspect of the Mother, the giant or ogre can symbolize that of the Father.

Gold dust running through fingers

To dream of gold dust running through one's fingers can signify regret at the ending of a close personal relationship (or of any other specially cherished experience), or at the speed with which children grow up.

Spiders

In dreams the devouring mother, who consumes her children through possessiveness or her power to arouse guilt, is often symbolized by the spider, who traps and lives off her innocent victims. The web woven by the spider to ensnare its prey is also a common dream image.

Sexuality

For Freud, unconscious sexuality lay behind much of our conscious behaviour, and he found sexual imagery to be the main driving force of dream symbolism. He believed that many acts of violence, such as those involving knifing and shooting, are associated with acts of rape: the obvious link is the brutal invasion of the body. He interpreted pre-occupations with asexual body parts as hidden wishes for abnormal sexual activity.

Freudians often associate mutilation with castration, and beating oneself or others, particularly small children, with masturbation. Riding a horse or bicycle, or chopping wood, or taking part in any rhythmical activity, connote sexual intercourse. The same meaning is attributed to climbing stairs or a mountain, the crashing of waves on the seashore, travelling, and the insertion of any one object into another, such as a key into a keyhole. Acts of deflation, such as a collapsing balloon, can refer to impotence; locked doors or windows are seen as representing frigidity.

In Jungian and other approaches to dream interpretation, sexuality, although important, occupies a less dominant position. Particularly in the Jungian approach, even explicit sexual themes may emerge as symbols of higher creative processes. There are strong cultural precedents for this: for example, the erotic sculptures that adorn the exterior of many Hindu temples refer not simply to the union of male and female but to wholeness within the self and to the marriage between earth and sky, mortal and divine, spirit and matter.

Fertility themes incorporating images such as corn, flowers or fruit may embrace a comparable hierarchy of meanings, from sensuality at one level to the fruit of the tree of life at another.

Red rose

As well as being the traditional symbol of love, the red rose in Freud's view often indicates the female genitalia, or the blood of menstruation.

Velvet or moss

In Freudian dream analysis, velvet and moss usually represent pubic hair. Other dream interpreters see in them symbols of a more generalized longing for the comforts of nature, or for gentleness, sensitivity or innocence.

Whips

Although whips in dreams can be a negatively charged symbol of sexual submission, more generally they can represent the dreamer's awareness of power, domination and obedience in relationships.

Knives

The knife or dagger is by far the most common male sexual symbol. It can represent the penis in its ability to penetrate, and can stand for masculinity in its associations with violence and aggression. It may also represent the "sword of truth" that cuts through falsity and ignorance, or the will to cut away false desires.

Quills and candles

Because they stand erect, quills and candles may often symbolize the penis. They may appear in dreams as general symbols of masculinity, or as representations of the Animus, the male aspect in the female psyche.

Gushing water

A flowing tap or faucet, or any other object from which water gushes, such as a freshly opened bottle of champagne, is often a symbol of ejaculation, representing the sexual act. It may also denote a new burst of creativity.

Cups

The cup is a classic female sexual symbol. However, because it may contain wine, and through its associations with the Holy Grail, a cup may also stand for love and truth.

Shoes

Some dreamers who report seeing shoes in their dreams associate them with sexuality: as with cups, hats and gloves, they can be entered by other objects, or by parts of the body. Women's shoes can sometimes stand for dominant female sexuality, which may come from the infant's experience of his or her mother's feet.

Hats and gloves

These items of clothing are often used by the dreaming mind to represent female genitalia. The obvious connection is that they enclose parts of the body.

Purses

The purse is among the most common of female sexual symbols. It can stand both for the female genitalia and the womb. As a purse can be both opened and closed, it sometimes represents the female power to give or withhold favours.

Anger and Frustration

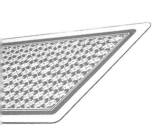

Anger is a powerful emotion that is often denied, repressed or misunderstood by the waking mind: hence its frequent occurrence in dreams. It is not always negative. Anger can represent valued aspects of psychological development such as courage, determination, leadership and self-assertion, and is also associated with the purifying effect of justified indignation. Even its more negative forms can be valuable when they erupt into dreams, because here their absurdity or destructiveness may become more apparent. Moreover, dreams will sometimes indicate areas toward which one's anger should more properly be directed.

Closely linked with anger, frustration is also a commonplace experience in dreams. We may find ourselves missing a train or an appointment, searching in vain for a parking place or for somewhere to leave luggage, or unable to read an important message or to convince someone of the truth of an argument. In all such instances, the dream may be reminding the dreamer of the need to discover the cause of his or her frustration, or to deal more effectively with it if its causes are known.

Amplification on frustration dreams may provide links with archetypes such as the story of Sisyphus, a Greek mortal punished by the gods by having to roll a huge rock up a hill for eternity: whenever he reached the top, the rock would roll back down, and he would have to start all over again. Such mythic archetypes may help the dreamer to come to terms with frustration, or to recognize that it is pointless to rebel against spiritual wisdom and the "gods" of the collective unconscious.

Frustrating tasks
Several major spiritual traditions deliberately frustrate their initiates, setting them pointless, never-ending tasks to eliminate the proud and tenacious hold that the ego has on consciousness. In dreams, apparently meaningless tasks (such as building a house of cards) may serve a similar purpose or may remind the dreamer that the ability to live with unavoidable frustrations is a sign of maturity.

Bottled-up feelings

A dream may draw attention to repressed anger or frustration by images such as a bottled-up gas or volatile substance, and to unbridled anger by flames roaring out of control. Unacknowledged anger toward particular people may emerge in dreams when the dreamer prepares poison for them, or defaces their photograph. Dreaming of decapitating a loved one is common when misunderstanding and arguments have brought anger and frustration into a relationship: the dream is not literally portraying the beheading of a partner, but is symbolically removing the source of a current problem.

Dam bursting

Anything that suggests a controlling force giving way before fierce energies from within can be a potent image of anger or frustration contained beyond the point of self-control. A flood blocking a familiar pathway may represent the dreamer's frustration, and may suggest the need to find an alternative and perhaps preferable route. In this way the dreamer is being reminded that there is often more than one way to deal with frustrations.

Loss and Bereavement

The need to continue with life, valuable as this often is in helping the mind to deal with painful experiences, sometimes means there is insufficient time to grieve over the death or departure of a loved one. In such instances, the dream may do the grieving for us. Images of loss, which often haunt the waking mind for many days after the dream, are part of the healing process, however unwelcome they may seem at the time.

Losing a treasured possession may also induce a real

Empty purse

The sudden discovery of an empty purse or pocket may indicate the loss not only of a loved one but also of the security that the old relationship offered to the dreamer.

sense of bereavement, and the dream may wish to emphasize this point. Loss of any kind may be symbolized by the despairing search for a friendly face in a crowd, or by themes of ashes or dust. Dreams may be steeped in nostalgia, providing warm or poignant images of a past way of life or occupation. Some part of the unconscious mind needs to repeat these experiences over and over again as an emotional safety valve until it can finally accept that the loss has really taken place.

A loved one receding

Distance is often used by the dreaming mind as a symbol of bereavement. A loved one may be seen receding into the distance, or waving goodbye from a far-off hilltop, or going out through a gate or doorway.

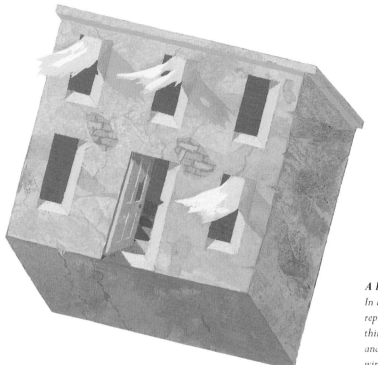

A house without lights
*In dreams a house often
represents the dreamer, or those
things that give life its stability
and orientation. Empty or dark
windows suggest the extinction
not only of the loved one but also
of vital aspects of the dreamer's
conscious life.*

Sometimes, bereavement dreams look ahead rather
than back into the past. The dreamer may see the loved one
in happy circumstances, or be visited and reassured by him
or her. Such dreams can leave the waking mind with
feelings of well-being, even elation, and in many instances
are so realistic that the dreamer feels certain of the reality
of life after death.

Amplification (see page 31) may provide links with
classical stories such as the loneliness of the nymph Echo,
who in response to her lovelorn calls received back only
the echo of her own voice. The dreamer may find such
archetypal precedents useful as a focus for dealing with loss.

Religion and Spirituality

Jung recognized the search for spiritual and religious truth, beyond our everyday material lives, as one of the strongest energies of the psyche, welling up directly from the collective unconscious – that vast genetic reservoir of myths and symbols that projects archetypal images into our conscious minds, especially in our dreams.

Religion and spirituality, more than any other themes, express themselves in "grand" Level 3 dreams. The "message" is often imparted through dream revelations that suddenly throw a clear light upon the past or illuminate the dreamer's way ahead. The dreaming mind may encounter the Wise Old Man, or other archetypal figures of wisdom, who reveal their truths and teachings. Other archetypes may take the form of symbols or religious icons. Transcendental experiences may occur, leaving the dreamer with profound feelings of exaltation and inner peace.

Level 1 and 2 dreams often depict the spiritual world in more immediate and practical terms. Dreams involving priests and other religious officials may represent the authority of the established church, while Old Testament prophets, Christian saints, Hindu avatars or Buddhist boddhisattvas may symbolize aspects of the dreamer's spiritual identity or aspirations.

Dreams that we may be tempted to interpret in sexual terms, such as climbing mountains or trees, may actually portray spiritual progress. A church, whose thrusting spire was seen by Freud as a phallic symbol, may represent the purified self or the richness and mystery of spiritual teachings. An eagle's soaring flight may signify spiritual aspiration, while a fall to earth could warn against the dangers of spiritual pride.

Amplification of spiritual dreams may usefully focus upon one of the creation or incarnation myths.

The Buddha
The Buddha taught that truth is found within, not without. His image in a dream often serves to remind the dreamer of the need to find the stillness at the centre of his or her own being.

Virgin Mary

The Virgin Mary embodies the divine feminine principle that appears throughout the religions of the world as a symbol of purity. In dreams, she often represents a supreme and selfless love or compassion, and the power that rules the heavens through grace and sanctity rather than though authority and strength.

Shiva

Eastern or other exotic religions have permeated Western culture, and thus may find their way into our dreams. For example, the Hindu deity Shiva Nataraja, Lord of the Dance, may appear as the dual aspect of divinity: he is the destroyer as well as the creator, paradoxically fearsome yet benign, dancing inside a ring of fire that both purifies and liberates.

Being of light

The being of light is an archetypal image that embodies a universal spiritual principle, relevant to all cultures and all religions. A figure is often shown bathed in light, or surrounded by a brilliant halo – a generalized symbol of divine energy, readily acceptable to the conscious ego.

Part II: Symbols

Contents

The Body

In ancient Egyptian, Greek and Roman and medieval European culture, the body was used as a metaphor for the spiritual world. This view is reflected in the maxim coined by the philosopher god Hermes Trismegistos, "As above, so below", and in the Biblical idea that God created man in His own image. Dreams also may link the body to the spiritual realm. The bodily condition of the dreamer or of other characters in dreams may reflect traits in the dreamer's psyche, or levels of psychological or spiritual progress.

Dreams make use of bodily symbols because these are images readily understood by the conscious mind, and because dream language, like waking language, draws many of its metaphors from material close to hand. Expressions such as the "foot" of a hill, a "yawning" chasm, or the "arm" of the law, relate the body to the outer world in the same way that a dream may use the symbol of the eyes to relate it to the inner world of the "soul", or use the metaphor of physical strength to denote the inner world of moral resolve.

The dreaming mind is not restricted by the conventions and laws of waking language, however, and can be extremely creative with its body metaphors. When we are asleep, our waking feelings of physical modesty and propriety are usually held in suspension, and our dreams may thus feel free to use symbolic images that would normally be disturbing to the conscious mind. For example, in addition to erotic images, the dream may show the inside of a human stomach, or show the intestines to symbolize "guts" or courage. And it may use the relationship between the body and the outside world in a symbolic way, taking hand-washing (for example) to indicate either the denial of responsibility, or purification, or alternatively to signify guilt or immorality which the dreamer may or may not be able to wash away.

Dreams may also allude to the body as a warning to attend to health problems, or as a way to express feelings about diet or exercise. For early dream workers, dreams of the body could reveal the future. Artemidorus (AD 170) wrote that for a man to dream that he is clean-shaven can indicate "sudden shame and problems", while Thomas Tryon, a nine-teenth-century English dream interpreter, insisted that to dream that one's belly is larger than usual foretells an increase in family or property, while seeing one's back in a dream predicts bad luck or (perhaps more obviously) the coming of old age.

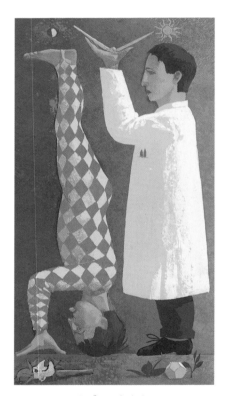

Left and right
For Jungians, an emphasis upon the right side of the body in dreams often refers to aspects of conscious life, while the left side represents the unconscious.

Hair

In dreams, hair often symbolizes vanity; conversely, the ritual act of shaving the head indicates a renunciation of worldly ways. Early dream interpretators suggested that to dream of going bald predicts an imminent loss of the heart. A strong beard can stand for vitality, while a white one can signify age or wisdom.

Bones

Bones can represent the essence of things. Being stripped or cut to the bone may signify a sudden insight, but also sometimes a deep attack on the dreamer's personality. Broken bones may suggest fundamental weaknesses.

Eyes

Eyes are symbolic windows into the soul, and clues to the dreamer's state of spiritual health. Bright eyes suggest a healthy inner life.

Heart

The heart carries archetypal significance as the centre of emotional life, and in particular as the symbol of love. Blood can connote the pulsing life-force, spilled blood its sacrifice and loss.

Mouth

For Freud, dreams about mouths may represent fixation in an early stage of psycho-sexual development, marked by immature characteristics such as gullibility or verbal aggression.

Teeth

Artemidorus interpreted the mouth as the home, with the teeth on the right side its male inhabitants and those on the left side its female. Teeth (falling out, broken, and so on) are the focus of many anxiety dreams.

Birth and Resurrection

Finding an egg

Discovering an egg, a baby, or a newly hatched bird, or any other image of birth, can indicate the emergence of new possibilities in the dreamer's life, and may also stress the need for careful nuturing.

The collective unconscious seems not to recognize finality, but projects instead a constant cycle of change. In our dreams, as in our myths, death may figure not as the end, but as part of an overall process of growth and transformation. Just as life is born from death in the material world (many of the world's religions celebrate the death and re-birth of the year as winter gives way to spring), so our psychological and spiritual energies constantly re-create themselves, assuming new forms in our imagination. Concerned with existence in all its aspects, the collective unconscious serves as a kind of channel through which new or renewed mental and spiritual energies constantly stream into the conscious world.

Dreams often enact re-birth and renewal by taking the dreamer back to childhood, overlaying old memories with new experiences. A dream that we are back in childhood may thus reflect adult concerns (such as the need for or the achievement of rejuvenation), rather than a wish to re-visit our formative years. Similarly, if we dream that we are older than we actually are, age may simply be standing in as a symbol for wisdom, or for rigidity, or for infirmity. These key principles of interpretation also apply when we dream about other people who are younger or older than in waking life.

Resurrection – the return to life of deceased people, animals or trees – is a classic dream archetype, often associated with new life suffusing old ideas or challenges. Alternatively, such dreams may warn of the return of problems that have not yet been laid properly to rest.

Birth, whether from the dreamer's own body (by way of mouth, belly or genitals) is frequently associated with new ideas and solutions, sometimes simply as wish-fulfilment, but sometimes as a clear indication of actual possibilities waiting to be explored.

The Divine Child

One of the most powerful archetypal symbols (see pages 34-8), the Divine Child represents perfection, re-birth, and the innocence of primal wisdom. Associated in many spiritual traditions with the virgin birth (a birth without original sin or the burden of karma), the Divine Child may symbolize the dreamer's own spiritual potential, ever-present beneath the dross of worldly concerns.

Nudity and Clothing

The female nude
Venus and other classical goddesses were often portrayed naked, or almost so. Such divine nudity was used as a symbol of love and sacred beauty, or in the case of the nine Muses it represented the divine truth of the arts. Nudity in a powerful woman, such as Diana the Roman goddess of the hunt, can help to suggest the Animus, the active principle in woman.

The Western tradition offers two strikingly different interpretations of nudity: on the one hand, childlike innocence; on the other hand, a profane and illicit attachment to fleshly pleasures. After falling from grace in Paradise, Adam and Eve covered their nakedness; shame had entered their consciousness, and the world could never be the same again.

In Level 3 dreams, nudity (like the archetype of the Divine Child: see page 38) can represent the dreamer's spiritual nature, or the authentic self. In Level 1 or Level 2 dreams, it can stand for a hierarchy of meanings spanning vulnerability, a desire to shed defences, a freedom from shame, and a love of truth. Excessive anxiety about nudity in oneself or others may suggest a fear of honesty and openness in relationships, or a failure to accept and integrate one's own sexual energies. For Freud, nudity could also represent a longing for the lost innocence of childhood, or an expression of the dreamer's repressed sexual exhibitionism, usually the result of punitive parental attitudes toward the dreamer during the self-display stages of childhood.

Clothing is similarly ambivalent. It can take the form of the brilliant garments of light worn by the saints, gods and angels, or it can stand for earthly vanity, an urge to deceive

Accepting nudity

To accept the nudity of others indicates the dreamer's ability to see through their defences and accept them for what they really are. Enjoying the nudity of others can indicate a love of naturalness and beauty, though in Freudian dream interpretation it tends to emerge as wish-fulfilment.

Nudity in children

Sometimes associated with the archetypal Divine Child (page 38), nudity in the young usually represents innocence, but can also stand for mischief or for love (Cupid). Attempts by the dreamer to cover up nudity in the young may indicate a tendency toward prudery, artifice and excessive rationality.

Others unconcerned about dreamer's nudity

To dream of being naked in a public place, among other people who are unconcerned about the fact, or oblivious to it, usually indicates that we should discard as groundless any fears that we will be rejected if our real self is revealed.

Disgust at another's nudity

To be distressed or disgusted by the nudity of another person suggests anxiety, disappointment or aversion at discovering their real nature behind the pretensions of the Persona. Where there is nothing inherently offensive about the body, the dream may show an unwillingness to let other people be themselves.

Armour
To dream of wearing heavy clothing or armour indicates that the dreamer is being over-defensive in his or her life. The dreaming mind may be indicating that with more self-confidence, openness and social ease, we would not have to take such extreme measures to protect ourselves from the outside world.

by appearances or to conceal shame or imperfection.

Although a cover for nakedness, clothes may by their cut, line or function draw attention to what they pupport to hide. Dreams about brassieres or trousers may therefore represent thoughts about breasts or genitals, or about maleness, femaleness or sexuality.

Clothing, particularly in auspicious colours, may represent positive aspects of the dreamer's psychological or spiritual growth, but when over-elaborate may suggest pretension, or a weakness for worldly display. Because clothes can make the wearer seem taller or thinner, richer or poorer, than he or she really is, they can stand for self-accusations of hypocrisy: a particularly flashy waistcoat or

tie may represent our knowledge that we are deceiving others in some way, establishing a persona at odds with reality. In Jungian interpretation, cross-dressing in dreams can indicate a need for, or warn of an exaggerated emphasis upon, the Anima or Animus (that is, the female side of a man, or the male side of a woman: see page 38).

Early dream dictionaries gave some curious interpretations, from which psychology is noticeably absent. A text of 1750 maintained that for a girl to dream of putting on new clothes presaged marriage, while in the *The Golden Dreamer* (1840) it is said that to dream of seeing a naked woman "is lucky; it foretells that some unexpected honours await you".

Over-tight clothes

Over-tight or constricting clothes usually indicate that the dreamer is inhibited or restricted by his or her public or professional role. More rarely, they suggest that the dreamer has ideas above his or her station.

Cloak

A particularly ambivalent dream symbol, the cloak can stand for illicit concealment and secrecy, for mystery and the occult, or for protective warmth and love. Freudian psychology typically associates the cloak with enveloping female sexuality.

Jewels

Jewels often suggest a valued aspect of the dreamer or of other people. Gold and diamonds typically represent the incorruptible true self, rubies denote passion, sapphires truth, and emeralds fertility. Jewels may also represent buried treasure, the archetype of divine wisdom hidden in the depths of the collective unconscious.

Underclothes

Underclothes may represent unconscious attitudes and prejudices, their colour and condition giving important clues about the specific qualities concerned. Feelings of shame at being seen in underclothes can indicate an unwillingness to have these attitudes made public.

Other People

We meet many other people in our dreams. Some are straightforward representations of people we know (such as lovers or colleagues), who remind us of our particular preoccupations; others represent, in a more abstract way, particular qualities, wishes or archetypal themes; others again stand for aspects of the dreamer's own self. Such is the condensed economy of dream symbolism that a single character can at times fulfil all three functions in the passage of a single dream.

Detailed analysis is often required before the exact function of a dream character can be identified; but, as with other areas of dreamwork, certain general tendencies are apparent. Jung established that a dream companion who appears in various guises in several dreams, but is recognized as the same character, represents aspects of the dreamer's real self. By reflecting in waking life upon the behaviour of this character in the various dream circumstances, we are provided with insights not only into the self but also into how the self may appear to others.

Conversely, Jung maintained that the frequent appearance of a dream character who is everything that the dreamer would not wish to be represents the archetype of the Shadow – the hidden, repressed side of the self (page 37). However, not everything about the Shadow is negative: by recognizing the Shadow we acknowledge our darker aspects, integrating them into consciousness; if we ignore the Shadow, on the other hand, our darker nature may appear again and again in our dreams, disguising itself in increasingly destructive forms.

Another archetypal character is the Trickster (page 36), who sabotages our efforts, but who may indirectly assist our development by challenging with paradox, and by revealing the absurdity of material pretensions.

Giants
In adult dreams, giants may represent recollections of childhood, when all adults towered above the dreamer. For children, they may represent present realities, such as the frightening side of the father. But although dream giants are awe-inspiring, not all of them are unfriendly. Some may symbolize the care and protection that the strong can give to the weak.

The Shadow
The archetype of the Shadow represents all that the dreamer wishes not to be. It is his or her darker side, the opposite of the Hero, and symbolizes hidden or repressed aspects of the self.

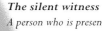

The silent witness

A person who is present in a dream but refuses or is unable to speak often represents an undeveloped function within the self. Jung saw such a figure as representing an imbalance between emotion and intellect, one overpowering the other to render it speechless or impotent.

The hero figure

Many of the most enduring fictional characters are popular because they personify universal themes and impulses, and dreams often use these figures as convenient ways of conveying archetypal messages to the dreamer. The Grail knights, for example, are archetypal Heroes, sacrificing themselves in the service of a higher quest; while Don Quixote plays the part of the anti-hero, a holy innocent who fails to integrate his inner ideals with outer realities.

The beautiful young woman

A beautiful young woman frequently symbolizes the Anima, the feminine principle in the male psyche. Often she may leave the dreamer determined that he must embark on a quest to meet her again – in reality, an inner motivation to discover the feminine part of hiself, and so unify the psyche.

The beautiful young man

A beautiful young man, often in the form of the hero, typically symbolizes the archetype of the Animus, the masculine principle in the female psyche (page 38).

Health

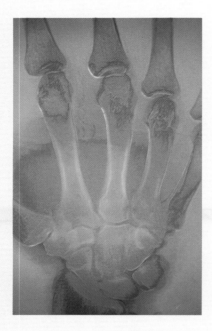

Fractured limbs
These represent a threat to the foundations of life, and to personal power. Or they may suggest anxieties about the safety of intimates.

Working in a hospital
This generally reflects a desire for a socially acceptable way of gaining control over the bodies of others (exemplified by the favourite childhood game of "doctors and nurses"). Being hospitalized may show a desire to relinquish control over one's own body or, in a different context, a fear of losing this control.

Change of weight
Weight loss typically represents the draining effect upon the dreamer of over-possessive or demanding people, particularly close relatives or colleagues. Weight gain or bloating may refer to our liking for flattery and may indicate that we are draining the life from others.

The Ancient Greeks and Romans believed that dreams could offer not only diagnoses of their ills, but also cures for them. It is possible that in cultures which emphasized this potential, dreams could indeed be an active source of medical help, just as they can be used today in other areas of problem-solving.

Some recent dream interpreters have believed that cures can arrive in dreams if the dreamer has concentrated on the problem for a long time before sleeping. Jung recognized that some dreams give clear messages concerning both physical and psychological health.

Bodily Functions

Toilet dreams

Excretion usually represents the dreamer's public anxiety or shame, or his or her urgent wish to express or unburden the self, whether for creative or for cathartic reasons. Menstruation can carry similar connotations, and is often associated with a sudden release of creative energy. To dream of unsuccesfully searching for a toilet may indicate a conflict between the need to express oneself in public and a fear of doing so; while to dream of finding a toilet engaged indicates jealousy of another's position or creativity; while causing a toilet to overflow indicates fear about losing emotional control, or failure to discipline creative potential.

Lack of privacy
If the dreamer is anxious that a toilet lacks privacy, it may indicate fear of public exposure, or a need for greater self-expression.

Freud associated dreams of excretion and toiletting with the anal phase of psycho-sexual development. The small child experiences erogenous satisfaction from excretion, and this experience, if insensitively handled by adults during toilet training, may leave the individual with permanent feelings of shame, disgust and anxiety over natural functions.

In Freud's view, anal fixation may even account for personality dysfunctions such as miserliness and uncontrollable rage. In certain circumstances, Freud also associated toiletting in dream symbolism with creativity.

Mortality

The collective unconscious takes the long-term rather than the short-term view, associating death with change rather than with finality. However, at an individual level, death has always vexed, terrified and fascinated us, and the Level 1 and 2 dreams that lie not far below the surface of our conscious minds may be filled with anxieties about our own death or about the ultimate loss of loved ones or close friends.

Fearful dreams about our own mortality may indicate the need for us to come more to terms, in conscious life, with our inevitable fate. Dreams about the death of others, though, may depict more abstract fears – for example, a concern about the annihilation of the personality or the self, or a dread of judgment or divine retribution, or of hell, or of the manner of death, and so on.

Death in dreams sometimes carries precognitive warnings about the future. Abraham Lincoln dreamed his

Funerals
Burial may represent the repression of desires and traumas, and may also denote an end, or the need for an end, to a particular phase of the dreamer's life. Where the funeral is not associated with someone known to us, it can be a reminder of the passing of time, of the irrecoverable nature of the past, or of the importance of not establishing too many emotional attachments.

own death only days before he was assassinated, seeing his corpse laid out in funeral vestments in a room of the White House. Many dreams of death, however, have no association with mortality at all. Some may relate to aspects of the dreamer's own psychological life, or to a change in life-circumstances. Symbols of death may also draw the dreamer's attention to forthcoming irrevocable events, such as retirement, losing a job, moving house, or ending a close relationship.

Reading the obituary of someone during a dream, or seeing their tombstone, or attending their funeral, may suggest the dismissal of that person from a job, or their relegation from the dreamer's affections, or their fall from grace in some other way.

Dream images relating to the dreamer's own death can carry similar meanings, although *The Golden Dreamer*, a dream handbook published in 1840, saw such images as denoting a speedy marriage and success in all undertakings.

Symbols of death

Medieval churchyards are replete with momenti mori *(reminders of mortality), and scholars of the time often kept skulls on their desks as objects of reflection. Hourglasses and the figure of the reaper are also important symbols. Dreams of such deathly paraphernalia may remind the dreamer that life carries a limited span in which to complete projects, or may point to forthcoming finalities such as the end of a marriage.*

Captivity and Freedom

Dreams often focus on the preoccupying conflict between the restrictions that life places upon us and our urge for freedom. Another common theme is our need to dominate others by holding them captive, possessing them, or placing them under some kind of obligation to us. Even a seemingly selfless desire to protect or nurture those closest to us, may arise from an unacknowledged self-gratifying tendency, in which service becomes a form of domination. Although it can of course symbolize more genuine motives, the urge to save others from danger frequently represents the dreamer's desire to secure their dependency or indebtedness. These motives can be shown more blatantly, as when the dreamer forcibly holds down or smothers another person, or withholds from them a key or some other means of escape.

Being tied up

Dreams of being tied up may indicate the dreamer's need for freedom, but were seen by Freud as a reflection of repressed sexual fantasies. These often date back to early childhood, and are involved with sexual domination by parents, or the urge to sexually dominate the parent of the opposite sex.

The dreamer's own need for freedom may be symbolized in similar ways, with the dreamer playing the role of victim and struggling to break free from others. Awaiting execution is a symbol for the most extreme curtailment of freedom, although in dreams it may relate to apprehensions about potentially auspicious events, such as marriage or the birth of a child.

Freedom and captivity may also symbolize aspects of psychological life that are being too tightly controlled by the dreamer, or which have been repressed into the personal unconscious and are clamouring for expression. Potential abilities that the dreamer is refusing to acknowledge may also be represented by captivity dreams , as may ideals and feelings that are being denied, or the urge to find meaning and spiritual purpose in life.

Domination

Bondage, of course, can have overtly erotic overtones in a dream,
reflecting sexual urges in the dreamer that are perhaps unacknowledged
by the waking mind. However, in a non-sexual context it can also suggest
repressed spiritual aspirations.

Setting free people or animals

Dreams of setting someone free may indicate the dreamer's altruistic urge
to serve that person by releasing him or her from psychological bondage.
Freeing animals from captivity more often relates to releasing the
dreamer's own emotions or primal energies.

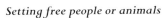

Climbing and Falling

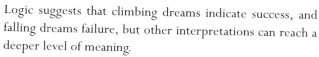

Logic suggests that climbing dreams indicate success, and falling dreams failure, but other interpretations can reach a deeper level of meaning.

For Freud, climbing dreams represented a longing for sexual fulfilment, but they also carry connotations of aspiration in other areas of life, such as personal or professional growth. Falling can symbolize failure or overweening pride, as in the fall of Icarus who flew too close to the sun, but it can also represent an abrupt and unsettling descent into the unconscious.

Tripping and falling, an experience that happens particularly during hypnogogic dreaming (see page 16), often emerges as a reminder of over-intellectualization, living too much in the head and failing to take care of the more basic or emotional aspects of life. Dreamers rarely report distress when hitting the ground: they either wake up just in time, or find the ground to be soft and yielding. Such dreams remind us that apparent disasters may often lead to no long-term harm.

Elevators
Elevators carry similar connotations to ladders, but usually suggest that the dreamer's ascent or descent is less the result of his or her own efforts than a consequence of chance and the actions of others. In some instances, the elevator suggests the rise of thoughts from the dreamer's unconscious, or a descent there in search of new ideas and inspiration.

Dreams of falling from a rooftop or from a high window usually indicate insecurity in an area of wordly ambition, such as a profession or social milieu. Falling from a burning building may suggest that the dreamer has been under insupportable emotional pressures as a result of his or her aspirations.

Amplification on climbing and falling symbols may provide links with mythological archetypes such as the Biblical story of Jacob, who saw angels climbing up and down a ladder set between heaven and earth. In the Renaissance, Jacob's ladder became an important Rosicrucian and alchemical symbol, usually shown with seven rungs (seven steps to heaven), representing the link between the physical and the spiritual self.

Climbing a mountain

Mountains are the male aspect, or on a loftier plane the higher self. They also suggest the self-determination needed if one is to reach the summit, as well as the dangers and the rarefied nature of the environment.

Slippery slopes

The quite common dream in which we attempt to climb up a descending escalator, a slippery slope or greasy ladder suggests failure to make progress in a desired area, and may serve as a reminder either to abandon the attempt or to seek a more appropriate way up.

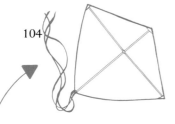

Flying

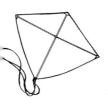

Flying dreams often bring a remarkable sense of exhilaration, and some dreamers speak of a strange recognition, as if flying is a skill that they have always possessed, yet for some reason have forgotten how to use. Rarely are flying dreams experienced as unpleasant or fearful, and the sense of freedom and exultation that they convey often open the dreamer's imagination to the infinite possibilities of life.

Dreamers do not always fly alone, but may be surrounded by friends or strangers, suggesting that others share their insight into the true nature of things. They may be accompanied by an animal or by an object, perhaps symbolizing important aspects of personal or professional life. Instead of flying under their own power, dreamers may find themselves in a vehicle of some kind, no matter how incongruous, or they may be leaping into the air on giant strides, like the three strides with which the Hindu god Vishnu measured the boundaries of the universe.

Flying a kite
To dream of flying a kite carries similar connotations to other flying dreams, but emphasizes the controlled freedom of some aspect of the dreamer, just as a kite is controlled in the wild natural forces of the wind. Such dreams can also stand for exhilarating but ultimately unproductive schemes.

Balloon
Balloons are associated most frequently with fantasy, the wish to escape, and the desire to rise above the conflicts of daily life. They can also represent a need to be more objective, far-sighted and all-inclusive in one's thinking.

Airplane
Flying in a plane often carries relatively straightforward associations, such as a wish to travel or see the world, but can also suggest a desire for rapid progress, or to achieve spectacular success in a particular enterprise.

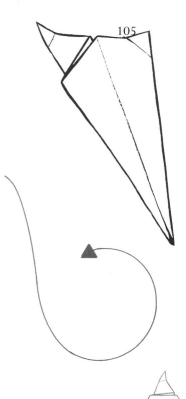

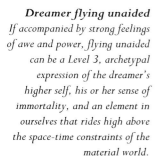

Dreamer flying unaided

If accompanied by strong feelings of awe and power, flying unaided can be a Level 3, archetypal expression of the dreamer's higher self, his or her sense of immortality, and an element in ourselves that rides high above the space-time constraints of the material world.

Flying in an incongruous vehicle

Often the incongruous object is something that represents comfort and security, such as a bed or an armchair, and the dream suggests a desire for adventure tempered by a strong predilection for ease and safety.

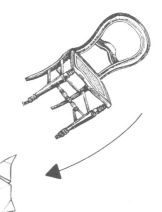

It is rare in dreams for flying to become confused with falling. Usually the dreamer floats gently to earth, having enjoyed panoramic views of the world below. On occasions, the descent may be by parachute, sometimes interpreted as indicating the safe resolution of a difficult challenge. Alternatively, flying may involve an element of delightful danger (as in hang-gliding), suggesting the wish to take more risks in some aspect of work or of a relationship. Being taken into the air against one's will, on the other hand, may indicate that the dreamer is being forced into too much risk-taking.

Travel and Motion

Freud was convinced that dream events incorporating travel or motion typically represent disguised wish fulfilments for sexual intercourse, the specific details of the dream providing clues to the dreamer's sexual tastes. However, travel and motion can stand for many other aspects of life, in particular for progress toward personal and professional goals.

The destination of dream travel may hold mythical or metaphorical associations. To travel westward may indicate a journey toward old age and death, while an eastward journey may signify rejuvenation. Travelling to Rome, where proverbially all roads lead, may indicate thoughts about fate, love or death. Other dreams about dying, symbolized in travel, may concern themselves with holding onto or letting go of luggage.

Jung noted the appearance in grand (Level 3) dreams of the archetypal quest for meaning and fulfilment, and it is certain that dreams of setting out on a journey are far more frequent than those of arriving at the journey's end. The dreaming mind reveals the need for progress in life, but indicates that decisions on ultimate goals must be taken at the conscious as well as the unconscious level: as these conscious decisions are made, so they are mirrored in the unconscious, and taken further in dreams.

Some dream images connected with travel reveal their meaning without much difficulty. Much is conveyed by the nature of the pathway that stretches ahead. An open road usually suggests new possibilities for progress, while a rocky path may indicate many obstacles. However, in keeping with Biblical imagery of the broad way leading to destruction and the narrow way to life, dream interpretation sometimes reveals that a seemingly difficult pathway is nevertheless the one to take. The scenery

Train journeys
Trains follow a fixed route, suggesting that the dreamer is receiving help on his or her journey. Being on the wrong train or passing one's destination can denote missed opportunities.

Stations and airports
These and other points of departure can indicate a plethora of possibilities, the meeting of ideas, or apprehensions or excitement about the future.

Car and sea journeys

Freud considered that the smooth motion of a car was a symbol not so much of sexual wish-fulfilment as of progress in psychoanalysis. Sea travel may represent a journey into the deep waters of the unconscious.

Crossroads

In dreams as in waking life, crossroads usually represent a point of decision. Depending upon the context and emotional charge, they can also symbolize a coming together of people or ideas, or a parting of the ways.

through which the dreamer is passing on the journey also reveals aspects of his or her inner life. To dream a journey through a desert, for example, may indicate loneliness, aridity, or a lack of creativity.

Further insights come from the means of transport: Jung noted that travelling in a public vehicle often means that the dreamer is behaving like everyone else instead of finding his or her own way forward.

Eating and Food

Eating has always been associated with sexuality. Freud recognized that the mouth is the first erogenous zone discovered by young children, and that throughout the lives of individuals with certain forms of personality fixation, orality may remain inextricably linked with sexual gratification, and may give rise to specific personality traits, such as verbal aggression.

Meat

In Nordic and shamanic belief, to eat the meat of an animal or adversary is to absorb its strength and energy. Freudian psychology suggests that for the modern dreamer this absorption is of one's own instinctive energies, which have hitherto been repressed or denied.

Even before Freud, however, dreams involving eating and food were often interpreted in sexual terms. Certain foods such as peaches and other fruits traditionally stood for lasciviousness, while others such as bread symbolized a more restrained, fertility-orientated sexuality.

However, as staples of life, food and eating demand a wider interpretation than the strictly sexual. Spoilt or bad-tasting food can suggest a sourness at the heart of the dreamer's emotional life; while waiting for a meal that fails to arrive can suggest neglect, emotional disappointment or lack of adequate support.

Social meals

Social meals that carry a positive emotional charge often reflect a confirmation of intimacy with others, shared interests, harmony, peace, and warm social relationships. Meals experienced as uncomfortable may represent frigidity, a threat to fundamental happiness, or social distance.

Types of food

As well as sensuality, fruit *can represent fertility in the creative arts or science (the bearing of fruit), or the receiving of rewards. Bitter fruits suggest that these rewards may not turn out exactly as expected.* Milk *usually represents kindness, sustenance and nourishment, whether physical or emotional. Freudian dream interpretation sometimes takes it to represent male semen.* Chocolate *or any other luxury food generally represents self-indulgence and self-reward. It may suggest guilt, and thus various experiences or indulgences which the dreamer feels should be resisted or denied.*

Picnics

Eating in the open air usually represents a desire for naturalness and simplicity, and for an escape from convention.

Fasting and gorging

For Freud, food often represented the two vital life-instincts — self-preservation, or greed, and species preservation, in other words sex. He saw the mouth, through which food enters the body, as the primary erogenous zone, and fasting and gorging as a symbol of sexual desire (denied or indulged). Fasting may also stand for self-punishment, perhaps because of guilt.

The dreamer's reactions to food can also be significant. Impressions of having over-eaten can variously represent greed, lack of discrimination, sensuality, or short-sighted behaviour. Refusal to accept food may suggest a desire to end dependency upon others, while providing food for others can indicate the urge to give support or to offer emotional involvement.

Vacations and Relaxation

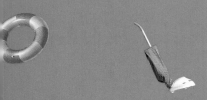

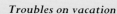

Troubles on vacation

Being on vacation yet still beset with trouble and anxiety frequently suggests an inability to escape from the responsibilities of normal life, however hard one may attempt to do so.

Isolated places

Seeking an island or a deserted place reflects a craving for solitude, or a conviction that most problems in life come from other people. Choosing to stay on an island can also suggest a wish to cling to consciousness instead of venturing onto the sea of the unconscious.

15:00

15:34

Most dreams are highly active, and it is rare to find oneself relaxing: a dash to the airport to catch a re-scheduled flight is a more likely image than lazing under a palm tree, cocktail in hand. However, dreams that symbolize a desire for relaxation, or that involve active preparations for potentially relaxing experiences such as vacations, are commonplace enough.

Dreams are realistic about vacations, and recognize that in many cases they can be highly stressful episodes. Thus, the unconscious mind may use vacation dreams symbolically – perhaps a particular vacation experienced in the past – to represent anxieties in other areas of the dreamer's life.

4:15

3:30

4:52

4:15

5:36

6:45

7:09

8:05

9:40

11:12

11:55

13:09

14:15

14:22

15:00

15:34

17:09

18:40

19:17

19:30

20:56

21:12

21:47

22:00

Packing for a vacation
Preparations for a vacation generally suggest a need to escape from everyday problems, or to seek new excitements and experiences. A wish to travel light can indicate a recognition of the unnecessary "baggage" that we usually carry with us throughout life. Anxiety about how much baggage to take away may represent a fear of, or preoccupation with, death.

19:17

19:30

20:56

Sometimes the dream contrasts the dreamer's own agitated state with the relaxed behaviour of people all around, emphasizing the subject's own need for stress-reduction. At times, the dreamer may feel intensely irritated by the inactivity of others, and this suggests a deep-seated resentment at receiving insufficient help in waking life, or anger at his or her own impotence. The dreamer may even find other dream characters reduced to dummies or dolls, and find himself or herself furiously but ineffectually trying to shake them awake.

At other times we may find that vacation dreams become confused with travel dreams of other kinds (see pages 106-107). For example, what starts out as a vacation may end up as a business trip or a duty visit to some friend or member of the family. In such dreams, the unconscious may be trying to indicate the dreamer's inability to engage in relaxing, light-hearted activities, and the puritanical or conscience-stricken impulse to turn away from enjoyment toward more earnest or dutiful pursuits.

24:00

Festivals and Rituals

From the beginnings of history, the cultures of the world have used festivals and rituals to celebrate important recurrent events, to honour the gods for maintainting life's course, and to mark the passage of time. Every society uses ritual to celebrate transitions in our lives, as we pass from one stage to another, from birth through puberty, marriage, parenthood and death. By sacrificing animals or enemies captured in battle, our forbears hoped to imitate nature's cycle of birth and death, offering the life of another so that their own existence could be spared and the gods could bring fertility to the earth.

Ritual is also a form of drama, and in dreams invites the dreamer to escape the confines of the conscious mind, passing into the fabulous world of the imagination. Performers may wear masks or special clothes, sing a

Fertility rites
Images of fertility rites in dreams often emerge from the collective unconscious. Jung saw them as indications of attempts to abolish the separation between the conscious and unconscious minds, and to forge a union between the dreamer and his or her inherited, instinctive self. Such rituals may involve sacrifice to a corn god or harvest deity, representing the death of the past so that future fertility and prosperity may be ensured.

particular song or recite ritual incantations to assume their new roles, leaving their everyday identities behind to enter the archetypal world of the unconscious.

Dreams associated with Christmas or other major religious celebrations can represent peace, generosity, goodwill, family and friends or, at a deeper level, a confirmation of spiritual truths. Wedding or other anniversaries can serve as reminders of transience, or more positively as indications of the significance of human and family ties, of the vows and undertakings associated with them, or – if the emotional charge is negative – of the restricting commitments involved. Dreams involving baptisms or christenings frequently represent purification, new beginnings, or the acceptance of new responsibilities. In Level 3 dreams, they can symbolize important initiations into new areas of wisdom or spiritual progress.

Weddings
A wedding often suggests the union of opposite yet complementary parts of the self, and the promise of future fertility. In the case of Level 3 dreams, it may be of archetypal significance, symbolizing the union within the dreamer of the fundamental creative forces of life – male and female, rationality and imagination, conscious and unconscious, matter and spirit.

Ritual renunciation
Any ritual that involves taking symbols of vanity from the dreamer, such as hair, clothes, or jewelry, may adumbrate the need for some renunciation of worldly power or pride, or of some aspects of the ego.

Art, Music and Dance

In various ancient cultures, such as those of Greece and Hindu India, it was believed that the arts already existed in another dimension, and that the task of the artist was to act as a channel through which they could enter into the physical world. Thus, the arts were always associated with the gods. The Greeks honoured Apollo, deity of music and the sun, and the Nine Muses, each of whom was responsible for one of the artistic domains. Hindus worship Sarasvati, harp-playing goddess of learning, while the poet Robert Graves attributed his poetry to a muse he called the White Goddess. Similarly, in dreams the arts represent not only the personal creativity of the dreamer, but also a way of access to higher levels of consciousness.

Sometimes we awake from our dreams with the dying notes of an exquisite melody in our ears. We may be unable to remember what instruments played, or what sequence of notes they produced, but we wake up uplifted and inspired. Such music usually comes from Level 3 dreams (page 23), and symbolizes the states of mind associated with higher levels of inner development.

Music

Beautiful music in dreams can symbolize the infinite potential of creative life, the heavenly "music of the spheres" that the Greco-Roman world believed could be heard by the human ear. By contrast, the chaos and confusion of discordant music suggests creative potential that has become distorted.

Painting

While successful painting can represent the dreamer's creative potential and even, at Level 3, the rightness of his or her vision of life, unsuccessful attempts can indicate creativity that still seeks proper expression, or reflects inner turmoil or uncertainty. Vivid colours may stand for unconscious energy, while drab ones can indicate the placing of a veil between the dreamer and the immediacy of his or her insight.

The eighteenth-century Italian composer Giuseppe Tartini dreamed that the Devil appeared to him, and played such a beautiful solo on the composer's violin that even the inferior copy recalled by Tartini upon waking (The Devil's Trill) is considered by critics to be his best work. The Greeks would have recognized the archetype that appeared in Tartini's dream not as the Devil but as Pan, the lustful fertility god, half-man and half-goat, who charmed the nymphs of heaven and enchanted mortals with the insidious music he played on his pipes.

If we dream of giving an artistic performance, this may be emphasizing our own unrealized potential, while being only an observer or listener may suggest a need to draw inspiration from others. Certain instruments, such as the harp, have always symbolized especially celestial qualities, while others such as wind instruments have often stood for more instinctive, sensual energies.

Because dreams draw upon the same sources as the imagination, they can provide artistic inspiration, yielding ideas, or sometimes complete pieces.

Musical instruments

Freud associated wind instruments with orality, and their appearance in dreams may indicate excessive gullibility or vocal aggression. A richer set of associations links pipes and reed instruments to Pan, fertility and the dreamer's natural instinctive energies. Trumpets may represent a call to awaken the dreamer's inner life. Drums can symbolize earth magic and altered states of consciousness, and have particular associations with the shamanic cultures of Siberia and elsewhere. Drums in dreams may also carry martial connotations or can represent extraversion or attention-seeking.

Dancing

In Level 1 and 2 dreams, dance can represent sexual courtship, or stand as a metaphor for sexual intercourse. In Level 3 dreams it often symbolizes awareness of the rhythms of life, the powers of creation and destruction (symbolized in Hindu culture by the dance of Shiva Nataraja), or the wild creative power of the imagination. It usually carries positive connotations.

Play

 To the small child there is no difference between play and work: all is simply activity, and the only distinction is between enjoyment and boredom. The dreams of adults retain this lack of differentiation. Thus, in dreams, play and games may symbolize work and other serious issues, just as work may emphasize the value of playfulness. Sometimes the symbolism resides in the objects used in dream play, sometimes in the nature of the play itself or its outcome, or in the other people who accompany the dreamer as playmates.

Dreaming of soft toys often represents comfort, security, or uncritical emotional support. The dreamer may be seeking an unqualified emotional acceptance by others, harking back to the relationships of childhood; or alternatively the dream may indicate a refusal to face reality, or may be registering a need for more natural or more tactile contact with loved ones.

Play symbols are open to a wide range of interpretation. Freudians, for example, link the rhythmical motion of playing on a swing with sexual intercourse, while others maintain that this can also represent the

Dolls

Dolls may represent the Anima or Animus, the qualities of the opposite sex within ourselves. Jung also found that dolls sometimes indicate a lack of communication between the conscious and unconscious levels of the mind.

exciting, unpredictable, varied nature of life, or may be reminding the dreamer of the zest and freedom of childhood. Dreams about board games frequently represent the dreamer's progress throughout life, with all its advances and set-backs. They may be wish-fulfilments, in which the dreamer competes and wins, or they may reveal a fear of competition.

 Dreams of play often emphasize that creativity carries a non-serious element, and that the best ideas come when the mind is in a playful, relaxed mood. Conversely, such dreams may suggest that the dreamer is taking serious issues too lightly, or that what seems an innocent diversion may be to others a matter of profound concern. Playfulness may also indicate that we are breaking certain rules upon which a relationship or some other important issue depends.

In Level 3 dreams, play may be linked with the archetype of the Trickster, or the Divine Child (pages 36 and 38), or may convey the message that there is an element of play in the universe itself, or that from one perspective the world is in essence what the Hindus call *leela*, the divine play that constitutes life.

Puppets

Glove puppets or marionettes suggest manipulation and a lack of free choice. The dreamer may discover that they stand as a symbol of the wish for power over others, or a lack of control in his or her own life, reiterating the cliché that somebody else is pulling the strings.

Toy trains

To dream of toy trains may represent our wish to assert control over the direction and power of our own life, even if this means reducing it to something restrictive, predictable and mechanical. The toy train may also suggest the dreamer's urge to return to the small, secure world of childhood.

Fighting and Violence

Violence in dreams is often strangely abstract, happening as if on film. Even if the dreamer commits an act of violence, the emotional charge may remain curiously neutral, which suggests that the dream is simply using physical violence as a metaphor for conflicts of other kinds — between theories or ideas, differences of opinion, or conflicts within the dreamer's own mind.

When the dreamer is the victim of violence, and the emotional charge is high, the dream may represent an assault upon status or relationships, or a threat to finances, health, or general welfare. If the subject enjoys watching violence in dreams, this may be linked to unacknowledged aggressive impulses within the self. In Freudian psychology, dream violence toward the father or mother is often associated with a wish to throw off authority.

Violence to the self

Violence toward the dreamer often represents a sense of guilt, and a desire for self-punishment, particularly if self-inflicted. It can also indicate that the dreamer is too vulnerable or apprehensive in the face of the outside world, as if outer forces are battering him or her into quiet submission.

Impotent weapon

Any weapon that refuses to fire in defence of the dreamer suggests powerlessness: the dream is indicating to us that we must find better ways of arming ourselves against the challenges of the world. For Freud, a gun or knife that refuses to function suggests sexual impotence, or the fear of sexual impotence.

Violence toward others

This often represents a struggle for self-assertion, or a fight against unwanted aspects of the dreamer's inner or outer life. Violence against a child can represent failure to accept the child in oneself, while violence toward an older man or woman may indicate a refusal to listen to the wisdom of others.

Wars and battles

Jung saw wars and battles as a sign of major conflict between aspects of the dreamer's conscious and unconscious minds. Such dreams are likely to reflect a struggle between deep instinctive forces and the rules of conscious conduct. They may indicate a need for reconciliation rather than victory.

Tests and Examinations

Examinations can be among the most stressful experiences in life, so it is hardly surprising that they make frequent appearances in our dreams. Among the most anxious of examination dreams is that in which we arrive to face a test without having done any revision, or must search frantically for the examination room long after the bell has rung to indicate that the start is imminent. The dreamer may find that the paper is written in an incomprehensible language, or may have to hunt despairingly for his or her name on a never-ending pass-list.

Dream examinations may stand for success and failure in any area of our personal or professional life. Failure in a dream test can be a highly uncomfortable experience, encouraging the dreamer to face up to shortcomings that he or she may otherwise have been unwilling to see.

Particularly when taking place in cold, impersonal surroundings, an examination can represent the remote powers of bureaucracy and authority that sometimes seem to control the dreamer's life, making arbitrary decisions that have a profound effect upon the future.

Facing an interview panel
Oral examinations can be even more anxiety-provoking than written ones. The interviewers facing the dreamer on the panel may represent aspects of the self, suggesting self-rejection or self-dissatisfaction. To be tongue-tied in the face of the panel may suggest that the dreamer has no convincing answer to the voice of conscience.

Giving and Receiving

Gifts that go wrong
Any dream image that appears exciting and attractive on the outside, but turns out to be rotten or repulsive within, suggests disappointed expectations, some kind of hidden agenda, or evil masquerading as good.

Giving is a symbolic form of social interaction and, as a dream image, provides clues about the nature of our relationships with others. Of course, whether the gifts are welcome or unwelcome is crucial to their meaning. Receiving many gifts on festive occasions such as a birthday emphasizes the esteem in which the dreamer is held by others, but if the gifts arrive at less appropriate times they can indicate the bombardment of unwelcome advice to which the dreamer may be prone.

Buying a present can suggest our wish to make a special effort for the person concerned, or more nebulously can represent our feelings of generosity toward them. If the present is particularly expensive, this may be a symbol of the dreamer's wish to make special sacrifices, or to help or serve the other person in an especially important way. On the other hand, showering presents on others, particularly if they are rejected, may indicate that the dreamer is being too thrusting in the gift of advice, lavishing attention where it is not wanted, or making inappropriate attempts to become acceptable to others. A gift that is never fully unwrapped typically relates to hidden mysteries, which the dreamer has started to unravel but for the moment remain at least partially unknown: the message is that with further perseverance such mysteries may be revealed.

A popular dream book of the nineteenth century suggested that to give a present in a dream foretells adversity; while if the recipient is a lover, this may indicate inconstancy or sickness in the person concerned.

Incongruous gifts
A gift that appears inappropriate to the dreamer, or causes feelings of unease, may indicate the unwelcome attentions of another person, or attributions, qualities or virtues in the dreamer of which he or she feels unworthy. If the dreamer is the giver rather than the recipient, the dream may be a reminder to present one's weaknesses — or true nature — more accurately to others.

Letters and Packages

Receiving goods or messages through the mail often heralds something unexpected in the dreamer's life, such as a new opportunity or challenge.

The dreamer's response to the contents of the package may give clues to the meaning. For example, failure to take a letter out of the envelope may suggest that full use will not be made of the chance on offer, while a sense of anticipation before opening it can indicate a more positive attitude.

Messages by mail
Freud regarded the envelope as a sexual female symbol. An unopened letter may thus stand for virginity, especially if it is new, pristine and white. If the dreamer is acting as mailman, or is carrying a message for someone else, this may indicate a potential for responsibility, or for being entrusted with secrets. It can also relate to our power to give or withhold pleasure from others, or to a dawning awareness of personal significance.

The identity of the sender (who often represents a part of the dreamer's unconscious which is trying to convey the message) may also be important to the dream's meaning.

To dream that a mailman is passing one's door without leaving a letter often serves to draw attention to the dreamer's disappointment, either over a particular issue or over the general direction of his or her life. If the dreamer runs after the mailman, this can indicate a latent determination to take a more positive attitude toward events, and to go out into the world and actively seek more exciting opportunities.

Rarely do dreamers report actually reading a message received in the mail: dreams prefer to leave such obvious resolutions to the waking mind.

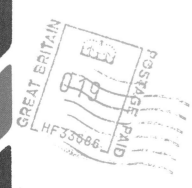

Shopping and Money

Stores and shops often symbolize the array of opportunities and rewards that we encounter in our lives. Our ability to seize them may be signified by the amount of money we dream we have in our pockets.

Store windows
To dream of seeing a store window full of attractive but somehow unattainable goods often suggests that the dreamer is excluded from the good things of life, but may also be reminding him or her to look elsewhere for more attainable, and perhaps ultimately more worthwhile, benefits. Jung found that dreams involving a chemist's or drugstore often relate to alchemy and the processes of inner transformation.

The dreaming mind may concoct any number of shopping metaphors to symbolize our ability or failure to take advantage of life's opportunities, or to find the solutions to particular problems. We may find ourselves in a store just before closing time, unable to find what is wanted before being shown the door. Or the shelves may be too high and the dreamer unable to reach up to them, or the possibilities on display so many and so varied the dreamer cannot choose between them.

Money generally represents power in Level 1 and 2 dreams, and to find one has insufficient to pay for what one wants can symbolize a lack of the abilities or qualifications needed to achieve some desired goal.

Hoarding money
Hoarding indicates both prudence and selfishness. Freud considered that it was a sign of anal fixation, but it may be an indication of insecurity. The sharing of hidden treasure can symbolize magnanimity.

Communication

Dreams are adept at revealing hidden fears as well as secret wishes and ambitions. Social vulnerabilities are particularly highlighted, and these may relate not only to the embarrassment of uncomfortable situations (reflected in many dreams of nudity), but also to the dreamer's inability to communicate effectively with others.

Generally such dreams portray the dreamer as unable to make himself or herself heard over the noise made by others, or as desperately trying to attract attention, or to alert others to what the dreamer sees as an impending disaster of some kind. But we may also find ourselves being laughed at, or hearing others making disparaging remarks at our expense. Others may turn away in contempt when we try to give opinions or advice, or to embark upon conversation. Sometimes the dreamer may find others tearing up something that he or she has just written, or pouring scorn upon well-intentioned efforts.

A particular feature of social vulnerability dreams is the image of the dreamer's failing to carry out a public speaking engagement of some kind. Being tongue-tied in front of an audience, or being ridiculed by those present, suggests fear of putting forward one's own ideas. Being asked to speak in a foreign language is an obvious reference to communication difficulties.

Unruly audience during public speaking
An audience that refuses to be quiet may relate not only to the reluctance of others to listen to the dreamer, but also to a general confusion of ideas, whether in the dream world or in waking life. The absence of an audience suggests a total neglect of the dreamer's ideas by others, or a complete lack of recognition of his or her achievements.

Rules and Regulations

Rules carry associations of structure, compulsion, control. If, in a dream, we seem to be giving strict instructions to others or to ourselves, then the dream may be drawing attention to a desire to make life less arbitrary and more predictable. If it is others who are making the rules, the underlying message may be the need for more discipline in life, or the need to be aware that one's direction is being circumscribed by limits imposed from outside.

Dreams in which we stand accused of breaking rules of whose existence we were unaware emphasize the unfairness of many life experiences. Such dreams may help to release the dreamer's frustration, or may signify that we have not fully come to terms with injustice.

Obeying rules can indicate that the dreamer is too easily led by others, but may also signify a valuable sense of loyalty and integrity. It is often helpful to explore the nature of the rules obeyed in dreams, as an aid to interpretation or amplification. The dream may be encouraging us to look more carefully at beliefs or conventions that we have been allowing to go unquestioned, or may be prompting us to be more objective in deciding where our loyalties should best be placed. To dream of arguing about rules may signify some kind of inner conflict.

Misbehaviour
Dreams in which the dreamer deliberately breaks rules often hark back to early childhood. The dreamer's natural urge toward self-assertion and testing the limits imposed by others may have been restricted by parents or other adults, and his or her rebellious nature may still lie repressed in the unconscious, asserting itself by dream transgressions.

At Home

Domestic events are among the most common subject matter for dreaming. Mostly, they occur in Level 1 and 2 dreams: these often incorporate apparently trivial events from the recent past (and especially from the previous day) which the dreaming mind has selected because it recognizes their value in symbolizing (and thus helping to access) significant material that is stored in the dreamer's unconscious mind.

When interpreting domestic dreams, it is important to look for anomalies between the dream material and waking experience. Often the dream is set in the dreamer's own home, or involves familiar domestic routines, yet some of the details are strangely inaccurate. Items of furniture may be in the wrong place, domestic implements or appliances may have grown or diminished in size, ingredients for cooking or materials for cleaning are nowhere to be found, and total strangers may suddenly appear and treat the house as if it belongs to them.

Anomalies of this kind are sometimes used by the dream to draw attention to particular wishes or anxieties, to unlock hidden memories, or to prompt a fresh approach to some kind of problem. By using them as stimuli for direct or free association (see pages 31 and 160), the dreamer can often without too much difficulty tease out the meaning of the dream, linking the everyday details to wider mythic, symbolic or archetypal themes.

Cooking

When food is being prepared for other people, this may indicate a wish to influence others, or make them dependent. If the emphasis is upon the food itself, the underlying meaning may be the dreamer's desire to mould some truth or insight into a more palatable form.

Cracked objects

Cracked objects suggest flaws in the dreamer's character, or in certain of his or her arguments, ideas or relationships. A cracked or broken vase or cup may symbolize lost love.

Occupations

Occupations feature prominently in dreams. Whether focusing on one's own trade or profession, or on that of other dream characters, such dreams usually relate to aspects of the dreamer's own personality. The workplace is a rich source of metaphor, embracing both objects and actions, upon which dreams draw freely to express their special purposes.

A visit to the optician, for example, may indicate a short-sighted approach to relationships or to other personal issues. We may find ourselves trying to sell newspapers to unheeding passers-by – a dream experience that may signify an inability to alert others to important information of some kind, and perhaps the need for a fresh approach. A dream of applying for a number of jobs could indicate a similar need, perhaps emphasizing that the dreamer will become increasingly frustrated unless he or she adopts a clearer sense of direction in life.

Often we may find ourselves dreaming of a current role or project, in which case the dream may be pointing out areas where we are functioning unproductively, or misusing abilities or letting new opportunities slip by.

Even those dreams that appear simply to re-live incidents from the previous working day are usually intent on providing clues about why things went badly or well, or suggesting how matters might be more successfully dealt with in future.

Waiter
If the dreamer receives (or gives) good service, this may emphasize the importance of inter-dependence. Bad or aloof service can suggest the need for more inter-personal warmth.

Police
Police can provide reassurance, but equally they may represent inhibition, and the censorship of natural impulses by the conscious mind. Being chased by the police can indicate the dreamer's need to face the accusations of a guilty conscience, or to learn from past mistakes.

Sailor
Owing to their connection with the sea and therefore with the unconscious, sailors typically represent the adventurous side of the dreamer, and the desire to explore unknown reaches of the inner self.

Bureaucracy
A dream of dealing with bureaucracy often relates to a lack of emotion, either in the dreamer or in those with whom he or she comes into contact. The dream may be urging a more personal and committed approach to relationships. Alternatively, it may be emphasizing the dreamer's helplessness at understanding complex issues, or perhaps signifying that it is necessary to pay more attention to detail.

Houses and Buildings

Houses in dreams usually represent the dreamer, and can symbolize his or her body or the various levels of the mind. Like bodies, houses have fronts and backs, windows that look out onto the world outside, doors through which food is brought, and other openings through which waste is later expelled.

It was from a dream of a house that Jung formulated his theory of the collective unconscious. The house was unfamiliar but undoubtedly his own, and after wandering its various floors he discovered a heavy door that led down to a beautiful and ancient vaulted cellar. Another staircase led to a cave, scattered with bones, pottery and skulls. He interpreted the cellar as the first layer of the unconscious, and the cave as the "world of primitive man" within himself that he termed the collective unconscious. Freud, however, interpreted Jung's dream as a form of wish-fulfilment, and found in the image of the bones and skulls a symbol of *thanatos*, the death-wish, possibly toward Jung's wife.

Other buildings can also represent the self. Courts of law, for example, may symbolize the dreamer's powers of judgment, and museums stand for the past, while factories or mills often relate to the creative side of the dreamer's life, emphasizing (depending on context) either its productivity or its mechanical, stereotypical nature.

Library
A library typically represents the world of ideas, and the ready availability of knowledge. To be distracted by other readers, or to fail to find a book, may indicate the need for more concentration or discrimination.

Place of worship
A church, cathedral or temple can represent the spiritual side of the dreamer, peace, or higher wisdom. To feel that one is a stranger inside a church may remind the dreamer to

pay more attention to the spiritual side of life. At other times, the dream may be warning of the need for more self-discipline or for allowing more time for inner exploration.

Door

A door opening outward may indicate a need to be more accessible to others, while a door opening inward can be an invitation to self-exploration. If a locked door proves frustrating for the dreamer, this may suggest that he or she should search for a new skill or idea to serve as a key.

Window

Freud interpreted both doors and windows as feminine sexual symbols; Jung associated them with the dreamer's ability to understand the outside world. Looking into others' windows (voyeurism for Freud) can suggest the dreamer is too curious about their lives, and perhaps uses this curiosity as a substitute for self-examination.

Rooms and floors

Like the mind, a house consists of different levels and compartments, all performing different functions and connected to each other by stairs and doors. In dreams, each room and floor can stand for different aspects of the personality or mind, which should be connected and integrated, but often are not. Generally, the living rooms of the house represent the conscious and preconscious, the cellars the unconscious, and the upper rooms the dreamer's spirituality and higher aspirations.

Unfinished house

As the house typically represents the self, an unfinished house or one in poor repair may be pointing out to the dreamer that work is required on some aspects of mind or body.

Castle

To dream of being inside a castle suggests security, but may also remind us that the very strength of our psychological defences may be isolating us from others.

Objects

Clocks and watches

Clocks and watches stand for the human heart, and thus the emotional side of the dreamer's life. A stopped clock indicates a chilling or stilling of the emotions, while a clock racing out of control suggests that the emotions may be overwhelming to the conscious mind.

The dream world is littered with objects, some familiar to the dreamer, some strange and unrecognizable. All have potential significance, and sometimes it is the more obscure things that provide the richest associations and amplifications in dream interpretation. However, not all associations are oblique, and some link clearly to waking experience. A camera, for example, often represents a wish to preserve and perhaps cling to the past, while hiding things in obscure places may stand for a wish for self-concealment. Similarly, a statue or bust often represents the desire to place someone or something on a pedestal, and may also signify their remoteness and unattainability.

A candle or torch suggests the intellect, or alternatively other, more spiritual forms of understanding, while a chest or casket can evoke various meanings, ranging from childhood (momentos) to forbidden knowledge (Pandora's box, from which the evils of the world escaped). The object's function is usually its most important aspect, although shape, colour and texture can also be significant.

Sometimes, like dream characters, objects may symbolize aspects of the dreamer's own personality, or aspects of family, friends or acquaintances. The dreamer may construct objects (well or badly), or destroy them, and discover during dream interpretation that these experiences provide insights into unconscious motivation or unacknowledged ambitions or desires.

A portrait or a still photograph often suggests the need to preserve a relationship, leaving it unchanged, or a desire to idealize the past. Sometimes the two dimensions of a photograph signify the dreamer's inability to see the deeper nature of a person or situation, making it difficult to enter into satisfactory emotional relationships.

Shells

The shell is a profoundly spiritual symbol that often represents the unconscious, and through its links with the sea, the imagination. It also stands for the divine female: Venus was born from a shell off the coast of Cyprus.

Books

Books variously represent wisdom, the intellect, or a record of the dreamer's life. Inability to read the words in a book indicates the dreamer's need to develop greater powers of concentration and awareness in waking life.

Garbage can

A garbage can frequently signifies unwanted memories or duties, or aspects of the self that the dreamer wishes to discard. It thus also suggests a desire for new beginnings.

Mirror

Seeing a strange face in the mirror often indicates an identity crisis. If the face is startling or frightening, it may stand for the Shadow, the archetype that represents the dreamer's darker side. Somebody walking out of a mirror may hint that new aspects are emerging from the unconscious, while an empty mirror can represent the clean slate of the dreamer's mind before the ego overlays it with wishes and self-images.

At School

School experiences are among the most formative in life, and appear frequently even in the dreams of elderly people. Sometimes the dream relates to specific happenings that still fill the dreamer with remembered pride or (more often) embarrassment, but sometimes it uses a generic school as a convenient metaphor to convey its message. Dreams of finding oneself back at school, but demoted to a lower class, or stripped of some coveted responsibility, symbolize childhood insecurities that have still not been resolved.

In addition to the school setting, school personnel may also feature in dreams. The school teacher is a classic symbol for authority, and may represent the father or mother, an elder sibling, or the dreamer's love for or fear of those who have determined the course of his or her life. Alternatively, a school teacher may stand for that censoring aspect of the dreamer's personality that keeps the more unruly impulses in check.

Dreams in which the dreamer is summoned to the headteacher's study may signify inferiority, guilt, or simply a dread of having one's misdeeds found out. Being publicly praised by a teacher, or being awarded a school prize, or winning a school sporting fixture, may illustrate the dreamer's belief, or need for belief, in his or her abilities.

Carrying a school bag
*A school bag full of books, pens and paper can, if carried happily, relate
to the dreamer's accumulated knowledge, and desire to continue
learning. If the bag is heavy or uncomfortable, this may signify that the
past is a burden, or that the dreamer feels weighed down by memories.*

The classroom

Typically, the classroom represents learning, and its life-long importance. It can also represent competition, public esteem or censure, or the need to re-think aspects of one's personal, social or professional concerns. The classroom can also symbolize nostalgia, or the dreamer's need to re-kindle the joy, passion or ambition of an earlier stage of life.

Ruined or dilapidated school

Any dream that returns us to childhood only to witness emptiness or decay suggests that we are carrying disappointed childhood expectations, or disquieting memories. Sometimes there is an added sense of the passing of time, the impermanence of life, and the need to look forward rather than dwell in the past.

Theatres and the Circus

All the dream world's a stage, a theatre in which magical transformations take place, images leap from the depths of the imagination, and the drama of life unfurls. Some dreams take this metaphor to its natural conclusion, using actual theatres, cinemas or circuses as their setting. Such dreams are usually imbued with a particular clarity and vivdness, reminiscent of the qualities of a "grand" dream (see page 30), using bright colours and an atmosphere of excitement and expectancy that mirrors the sense of anticipation we experience in such settings in our waking life.

A dream theatre is an illusion within an illusion, and may appear to offer the dreamer an understanding of the mystery that lies behind the world of appearances. However, the dreamer may also find the theatre or circus ring empty, or the cinema screen blank, and experience a haunting loneliness, as if he or she is excluded from the revelation that is about to appear to others.

If we actually finds ourselves on the stage, or in the circus ring, participating in the drama, it may be that we identify with the character or aspect of behaviour on display. But if the dreamer is merely an onlooker, this may indicate a danger of being taken in by the powers of illusion or, depending on the context, an unfulfilled wish to throw off the conventions of ordinary existence and become part of the more instinctive, colourful and exciting world symbolized by the performance.

Actors may represent other people of importance in the dreamer's waking life, or they may invoke the archetype of the Persona, the mask that we assume to confront the outside world. The interplay of humans and animals may carry particular significance, relating to the interaction between the conscious, rational mind and the unconscious, instinctive mind.

Clown

The clown is an aspect of the archetypal Trickster, making a fool of himself or herself to mock the pretentiousness and absurd posturing of others.

Acrobat

The acrobat represents the combination of strength and grace, and thus the union of male and female. Trapeze artists may signify spiritual courage, demonstrating to the dreamer that only by risking one's own safety can true inner progress be accomplished.

Lion tamer

Like the Strength card in the Tarot pack, which shows a beautiful young woman holding a lion's jaws apart, the dream image of the lion tamer demonstrates that the wildest of beasts can be tamed by gentleness and persuasion, as much as by force. By dominating the king of the beasts, the lion tamer symbolically triumphs over his baser instincts, not by repressing them but instead by bending them to his will.

Fire-eater

The fire-eater may represent the fierce, angry aspect of the self, but may also indicate the possibility of controlling this aspect. He often stands for effectiveness, mastery, the outrageous action that overcomes difficulties.

Conjuror

The stage conjuror is the master of illusion, performing by trickery acts of transformation that might take the genuine magician a lifetime to achieve. He is thus the master of the short-cut, and unexpected solutions, but also of cunning and deceit.

Ring-master

The ring-master commands the skills of both humans and animals, yet performs no acts himself. He thus feeds upon others, and his presence in a dream may indicate the ultimately barren nature of this kind of power.

Performing animals

As representatives of base instincts, tame animals symbolize the extent to which man can work with his more primitive self, to produce results beyond the scope of the conscious mind.

Towns and Cities

Just as the house stands for the self in Jungian psychology, so the town or city represents the community, the social environment beyond the self, including family and friends, and the whole network of responsibilities which inevitably enfolds us (like a network of streets radiating from a square or market place).

A busy town, or one with doors and windows open, or bustling cafés, may represent the warmth of the dreamer's relationships with others; while a town with wide, empty streets or vast, desolate piazzas can indicate a sense of isolation or rejection from society.

A large, impersonal city may suggest that the dreamer

Walled city

A wall around a city, or around an individual house, suggests exclusiveness, a wish to keep others out, but also a desire to protect one's treasured possessions. The dream may be suggesting that such a wall is necessary if social values are to be maintained, or it may be inviting the dreamer to recognize that a wall already exists and to ponder upon its implications and the extent of its usefulness.

has many acquaintances but few close friends, and the dream may be offering coded advice about the need to establish more intimate relationships.

If the houses themselves are vague and shadowy, this may suggest the dreamer's lack of understanding of other people, or perhaps lack of self-knowledge.

A city beneath the ground or the sea typically relates to the dreamer's unconscious, and suggests that far from leading us away from our fellow men and women, deeper self-knowledge allows us to recognize the common links that we share with them through the collective unconscious.

Town on a hill

Typically, a town or city on a hill, particularly if it appears in a Level 3 dream, suggests wisdom, heaven, the home of the gods, the stronghold of the righteous. The image may suggest a goal or an ideal toward which the dreamer is striving, and may provide reassurance that such ambitions are ultimately attainable.

Ruined city

Ruins tend to suggest neglect and decay rather than deliberate destruction. A ruined city may be drawing the dreamer's attention to a neglect of social relationships, or of aims or ideals in life that were formerly more steadfastly kept in mind.

Harbour

A harbour in a dream is almost always a point of departure. It may represent people whom the dreamer has to leave behind, as he or she sets out into the unknown waters of the unconscious, or aspects of the dreamer's self that similarly have to be abandoned.

The Elements and Seasons

The elements and the seasons are frequently associated with Level 3 dreams, because they relate to the natural energies and rhythms of life and thus serve as powerful symbols both of the dreamer's own being and of significant life changes. Astrologers use the elements to symbolize the four essential qualities of mankind: Earth for fertility and steadfastness, Fire for ambition and the will, Water for the imagination, Air for intelligence.

Rivers and streams are particularly potent metaphors for the passing of time, and dreams of standing on the river bank may suggest that it is time for the dreamer to pause and reflect upon the direction and intensity of life. Rivers may also serve to remind the dreamer that it is possible to "flow" past obstacles that lie in the way, rather than confront them directly, and that like a river life alternates between hectic rapids and deep slow-moving pools, shallows and depths. Water is a potent symbol of the unconscious, and attempts to dam a river, or stem the leak from a pipe, may indicate that the dreamer is trying to repress material that is flowing from the unconscious mind.

Rainbows
Universally auspicious symbols, rainbows stand for redemption, good news, promise and forgiveness. In Level 3 dreams they can be associated with the magical quest for the treasure of self-knowledge, or for the bridge between heaven and earth that awaits the enlightened mind.

The sea
Jung believed that turning to face the sea indicates that the dreamer is prepared to confront the unconscious, while creatures emerging from the deep represent powerful archetypal forces. For Freud, the sea and the incoming tide were primal symbols of sexual union.

Snow
Melting snow suggests fears and obstacles dissolving in the dreamer's path, but snow can also symbolize transformation and purification. Ice can indicate petrifaction, a halt to progress, or an obstacle in the way of the creative flow of the dreamer's mind. It may also represent a lack of emotional warmth, a suggestion that the dreamer has paid insufficient attention to his or her feelings.

Lightning
Lightning suggests inspiration, but warns the dreamer that flashes of brilliance can also be destructive. Lightning and thunder can also be reminders of the awesome power of nature, and of the forces that lie beyond the dreamer's conscious control.

Spring is an obvious signal of new beginnings, while high summer indicates achievement and the need to savour life's pleasures instead of always hurrying by. Summer also symbolizes the conscious mind, far-sightedness and clarity of thought. Autumn and winter represent the unconscious and the darker, hidden side of the dreamer's self, but may also indicate that a fallow period is called for, a time of incubation before new ideas burst

forth. Autumn and winter can also denote that even in the midst of apparent death, life goes on, working its mysteries unseen until the time for regeneration and re-birth.

Rain often represents the illusory nature of opposites, such as water and air, the imaginative and rational parts of the mind. It often underlines the importance of harmonization between apparently disparate elements of the dreamer's inner and outer life.

Alchemy symbol

This diagram, from a seventeenth-century alchemical manuscript, represents the universe. At its centre is the "fifth essence", the mystical power that binds the four elements together, and has been known to appear in dreams.

Fire

Fire consumes but also purges. In dreams it suggests the need for sacrifice, but at the same time promises to open up new opportunities. Fire is a masculine energy, and represents that which is overt, positive and conscious. Out of control, however, it suggests the need for the dreamer to take better charge of unbridled passion or ambition.

Earth

Dreams of sitting or lying on the ground suggest the importance of realism, an end to over-extravagant flights of fancy. The earth can also symbolize fertility, and like water can represent the feminine. Barren earth can hint that new ideas are imminent: the old ground must be ploughed up and sowed with the seeds of new life.

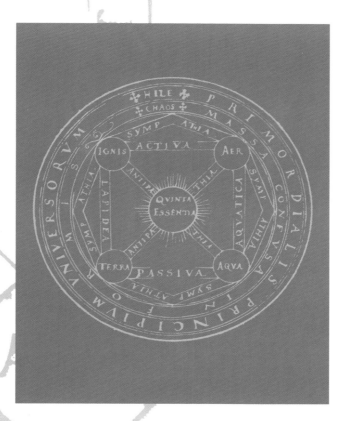

Air

Air is associated with wisdom lightly worn, and clarity of thought. We may find ourselves bounding in great leaps across the countryside, or floating gently down to earth, or travelling in a balloon or on a cloud. Air is the element that symbolizes otherworldly concerns, but the dream may also be warning of the dangers of losing contact with reality.

Water

Water is the symbol par excellence *of the unconscious, the depths of the imagination, the source of creativity. To dream of swimming suggests that the dreamer should venture into this realm, but if he or she struggles to float, this may be a warning that more caution and more careful preparation are required.*

Animals

Animals are particularly power-ful dream symbols, and usually carry a universal meaning, although they can also appear as specific animals known to the dreamer, in which case their significance tends to be personal. As well as real animals (general or specific), dreams may also make use of animals encountered in films, myths or fairytales. Sometimes, too, there may be a reference to animal associations embedded in the similes and clichés of idiomatic language (linking foxes with cunning, elephants with long memories, pigs with gluttony, and so on).

Animals have always signified our natural, instinctive and sometimes baser energies and desires, and in dreams they often draw our attention to undervalued or repressed aspects of the self, and put us in touch with a source of transforming energy deep within the collective unconscious. Devouring an animal can represent the assimilation of natural wisdom, just as in Nordic myth

Butterflies

Butterflies have often been used to symbolize the soul and its transformation after death. Taoist mythology preserves the story of sage Chuang-Tzu who was unsure whether he was a man who dreamed one night that he was a butterfly, or a butterfly now dreaming it was a man.

Siegfried learned the language of animals after eating the heart of the dragon Fafnir.

Animals in dreams may be frightening or friendly, wild or tame, and their demeanour can be an important clue for interpretation. They may even speak or change their form. In the native American tradition the shaman (spiritual magus) seeks a power animal in dreams, who will then act as a wisdom guide during the shaman's journeys to other worlds.

A dog can represent devotion, as symbolized by Argos, the first creature to recognize the Greek hero Odysseus when he returned from his wanderings, but it can also stand for the destructive force of misused or neglected instincts, just as the hounds of the Greek hunting goddess Artemis tore Actaeon to pieces when he invaded her privacy. Cats are among the most common dream animals, and often stand for intuitive feminine wisdom and the imaginative power of the unconscious.

Horse

The horse generally symbolizes mankind's harnessing of the wild forces of nature, while a winged or flying horse can represent the unleashing of energy for psychological or spiritual growth. In Freudian dream interpretation, a wild horse represents the dreaded, terrifying aspect of the father.

Wild beasts

Freud considered that ferocious, untamed animals represent passionate impulses of which the dreamer is ashamed; the more numerous and diverse the animals concerned, the more varied and threatening these impulses may be.

Lion

The lion almost invariably appears in dreams as a regal symbol of power and pride, and often represents the archetypal, powerful and admired aspect of the father.

Fish

Fish have commonly been used to symbolize divinity, and often stand for the spiritual abundance that feeds all men and women. In dreams they can also represent insights into the unconscious. Fish caught in a net and brought to the surface represent the emergence of these insights into the full light of consciousness.

Birds

In most cultures, birds symbolize the higher self, although small birds who stay close to the earth represent more accessible instinctive wisdom. The dove frequently stands for peace and reconciliation.

Monkeys

Monkeys often represent the playful, mischievous side of the dreamer, and may symbolize an immature yet instinctively wise aspect of the dreamer's consciousness that may require expression. In the East, the monkey can also symbolize the untamed, chattering mind that needs to be stilled by meditation.

Numbers and Shapes

One

One is the prime mover from which all manifest creation flows, the single principle from which diversity is born. In dreams it may represent the source of all life, the ground of being, the still centre of the turning world, or the expression in tangible form of the emptiness of the circle.

Four

Four is the number of the square, harmony, and the stability on which the world depends. It relates to the four seasons, the four directions, the four elements (earth, air, fire and water) and Jung's four mental functions of thought, feeling, sense and intuition.

Popular dream interpretation has always placed great significance upon the occurrence of shapes and numbers.

Jung noticed the prevalence of archetypal shapes such as circles, triangles and squares in the dreams and doodles of his patients. As his clients began to progress toward psychological health, mandala-like shapes and designs, with squares and circles radiating from a central point, began to feature with increasing prominence in their dreams. Jung saw striking similarities between these geometrical patterns and the religious diagrams that Tibetan Buddhists use as a focus for concentration when they meditate.

Once Jung had identified this geometrical archetype, he found its equivalents in all the myths and belief systems of the world. The mandala seemed to him like a map of the integrated human mind, reflecting in its growing beauty and complexity the development of the psyche toward wholeness.

Numbers also represent archetypal energies of the collective unconscious, and play a major role in the world's symbolic, mythological and occult traditions. Various cultures subscribe to the idea that numbers such as three and seven are divine, and their appearances in dreams have been taken to be revelations from the gods. For Freud, dream numbers were usually "allusions to matters that cannot be represented in any other way".

Numbers in dreams may not be given directly (though this is by no means uncommon). In dream recall the dreamer may be aware that objects or characters were presented in certain numerical patterns, or that actions tended to be carried out a set number of times. Dream interpretation and amplification can then focus upon these numbers and identify the significance that they carry for the individual dreamer.

Two

Two is the number of duality, divine symmetry, and balance. It represents the coming together of male and female, father and mother, and of the opposites that emerge from the one and define the created world.

Three

Pythagoras called three the perfect number: it is the number of synthesis and the three-fold nature of mankind, the union of body, mind and spirit. Three is also the symbol of the active creative force made manifest in father, mother and child and in the Holy Trinity.

Five

This is the number of the pentagram, the five-pointed star that represents mankind, the link between the heavens and the earth, with feet on the ground, arms reaching toward the horizon, and head in the skies.

Six

Six represents perfection. It is the number of love, and in dreams it stands for a movement toward new understanding and inner harmony.

Seven

In Christianity and Hinduism, seven is the number of God, the mystical number. In dreams, it is the number of risk and opportunity, and of the power of inner transformation.

Eight

This is the symbol of the initiate, of the Buddha's noble eightfold path, and of regeneration and new beginnings.

Nine

Nine is the number of indestructibility and eternity, of three multiplied by itself. It has the remarkable property that its multiples always reduce back to the number nine, from which they came: 18 (9x2), for example, if added together (1+8), makes nine, as does 72 (9x8), 81 (9x9), and so on.

Ten

This is the number of the law, the ten commandments, and the incarnations of the Hindu god Vishnu, protector of good and destroyer of evil.

Eleven

Eleven is the beginning of a journey, although for some it is the number of transgression. It reminds the dreamer that a new beginning (1) need not be an abandonment of what has already been learned (10).

Twelve

Twelve is the number of a new spiritual order. There are twelve disciples of Christ, earthly holders of spiritual truth, and twelve signs of the zodiac.

Zero

The zero or circle represents infinity, the void, the unmanifest, ineffable and unknown emptiness from which the multiplicity of life was created and to which it ultimately returns. It can also signify the female principle, entry into the mysteries, or a sense of completion.

Colours

People woken during episodes of REM sleep almost invariably report that they have been dreaming in colour. The colours themselves are often one of the most revealing aspects of dream imagery, and colour is also a key element of all the major symbolic systems of the world. People who claim normally to experience only black and white dreams probably repress memories of colour in the brief moments after waking.

As with other dream symbolism, the meaning of particular dream colours varies from one individual to another, depending upon the particular associations held in the unconscious, although universal meanings also come into play. The primary colours are usually most significant. Violet, a combination of the primaries red and blue, has an especially mystical, enigmatic quality, suggesting at one and the same time a union and a tension between the dual creative forces behind the universe.

Traditionally, gold and silver stand for sun and moon, masculine and feminine, day and night. For Jung, these hues represented the conscious and unconscious levels of the mind, and their juxtaposition suggested the path toward psychic wholeness.

Brown
Brown usually represents the earth, but for Freud was a symbol of anal fixation.

Red
Red is the colour of vitality, passion, anger and sexual arousal. Red wine is often associated with excess and sensuality, but at a deeper level can represent the altered states of consciousness associated with Dionysos, the Greek god of divine ecstasy.

Orange
Orange is the colour of fertility, hope, new beginnings, and the dawning of spirituality.

Yellow
In Chinese symbol systems yellow was sacred to the Emperor, and in dreams this colour can represent the wise use of authority and power. Conversely, as in the saffron robes of the Buddhist monk, it can represent humility, and the importance of service.

Green
Green is the colour of nature, the elements and the forces of regeneration, bringing new life from the death of the old.

Blue
Blue is usually a highly spiritual colour when it appears in our dreams, suggesting the infinity of the sky and space, and the robe of the Queen of Heaven, the symbolic form of the Virgin Mary.

Sounds and Voices

Dream sounds should not be neglected during interpretation. Music especially tends to be laden with meaning. It may be that a melody has personal associations, or it could be the title or the lyrics (even when the words are left unsung) that are significant. Alternatively, music may carry a message of its own, even when the melody is unrecognized or not remembered upon waking. For example, it can denote a beguiling danger, like the flute-

Bugles
Traditionally the sound of the trumpet is a call to arms or action, suggesting that the dreamer must arouse his or her hidden potential, or must become more alert to the pressing necessities of life.

Whistling
Surprisingly, whistling sometimes carries magical overtones, as when the sailor whistles for a wind. Another possible connotation is the link between humans and animals, as in a master's call to a dog.

playing of Pan, which enticed mortals from rationality into the primitive world of nature. The harp and other stringed instruments (sounds coaxed as if from nowhere, without the help of breath) may be images of the spiritual side of the self. Strange, half-heard voices can have something of the same mystic quality, often suggesting that the dreamer must listen more to the promptings of inner wisdom.

Ghosts and Demons

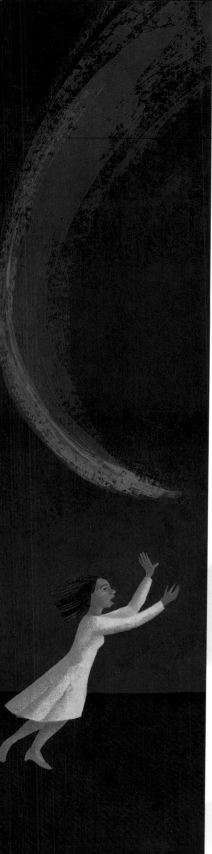

The witches, vampires, werewolves and half-seen ghosts of children's dreams often symbolize those aspects of the self that the child is unable to understand or integrate into his or her world-view.

If childhood monsters persist into the dreams of adulthood, it could be that the work of comprehension and integration remains uncompleted. The dreamer, fearful of forces beyond the reach of the conscious mind, may be still trying to reduce reality to safe and predictable dimensions.

As with all nightmares, such dreams serve the purpose of urging the dreamer to turn and face the pursuing dark forces, and to see that it is only fear that turns them into monsters. By recognizing and accepting the many energies that make up our psyche, we may in time come to a better understanding of our conscious and unconscious minds, where most of the mysteries of life reside.

The Tibetans often equate monstrous dream images with wrathful demons and guardian deities – the powers within the self that, properly used, can deter and destroy ignorance, illusion and false motivation. One nineteenth-century text on dream interpretation even considered that to dream of ghosts and spectres was actively propitious, foretelling the advent of good news from distant places. To try to see a monster as a potentially beneficent force can sometimes help when more obvious interpretations fail.

Ghosts and spectral figures
The image of a ghost as a shadowy, insubstantial being may suggest knowledge within the dreamer that now requires fleshing out and empowering by the conscious mind. Such images may also suggest fear of death or of an after-life bereft of sensation and human emotion. Dreams of ghostly figures hovering over the dreamer's sleeping body are sometimes interpreted as OBEs (Out of the Body Experiences), in which the dreamer's "soul" or dreaming body appears to shed its physical form.

Giants

The monster or giant who towers over a small and vulnerable child is an archetypal theme in children's dreams and stories. Such figures often represent adults in the child's life who dominate him or her with what must seem an arbitrary and near-infinite power. By confronting these monsters in their dreams (and therefore in the unconscious), chidren can come to terms with them in their emotional lives.

Impossibilities

Dreams are not bound by the rules of waking life, but operate in the world of the imagination, reminding us that our normal way of perceiving reality is only one of many possible states of consciousness. Reminiscent of the Zen Buddhist *koan* technique, which asks the initiate impossible questions, dreams may deliberately distort waking reality, "shaking" the dreamer's mental kaleidoscope, and producing new juxtapositions of ideas and experiences, which give rise to new patterns of thought or behaviour.

When a dream presents material that appears impossible to the waking mind, this very incongruity may be the crux of the meaning. One manifestation of this is the reversed relationship. A platform, for example, may move toward a train instead of vice versa, perhaps emphasizing to the dreamer that it is necessary to approach life from a completely new perspective. The dreamer may appear in

Absurdities

Cars or trains moving on water, ships sailing on land, the dreamer swimming through a cornfield: these are all examples of how dreams juxtapose seemingly incompatible elements. Sometimes such incongruities are designed to remind the dreamer that there are infinite possibilities in life — be more adventurous.

Talking paintings

Dreams in which the characters in a picture
talk or come to life usually relate to the
dreamer's imaginative powers, and may
emphasize ways in which fantasies help or
hinder his or her psychological development.
If saturated with the numinous quality of a
Level 3 dream, such experiences often serve to
confirm the dreamer's inner progress.

the opposite sex, drawing attention to his or her neglect of the Anima or Animus, the female aspect of man and the male aspect of woman. Winter and summer may be combined or reversed, flowers may bloom in a snowfield. Such reversals may sometimes be aiming to teach the dreamer that seeing everything in terms of opposites (including forces at war within the dreamer's mind) is limiting: only by uniting our various energies can we realize our full potential.

Transformations

We live in a world where transformations dance around us like shadows on a sunny, wind-swept day. The endless alternation of the seasons, the cycles of earth and sun, the young growing old, the present melting into the past, are inextricably bound up with our lives.

Our perceptions of this continually changing world are as unstable as the world itself. Objects appear subtly different each time we look at them, depending on the angle of view, on our mood of the moment, on our level of attention, and on tricks of the light. The same pattern of ebb and flow affects our perceptions of ourselves and others, and especially our apprehensions of personality and of character.

It is not surprising, therefore, that transformations also play a major role in our dreams. Often they serve as a kind of shorthand, a bridge passage between one dream subject and the next, and linking images together in the way that a dissolve does in a film. Equally, they can be meaningful in their own right, drawing attention to profound relationships between different aspects of our lives, and between the various preoccupations of the unconscious.

Dreamer transformed into a plant
To become a plant (or a tree, like Daphne in Greek myth) is normally an image of nature and integration, although for some dreamers the loss of mobility might be significant.

Sometimes a whole scene will transform itself into another, like a vision conjured by an enchanter. It is relatively commonplace too for the dreamer himself or herself to change — for example, from man to woman, from young to old, from victor to victim.

In the process of dream analysis, transformations can sometimes provide the most important clues. An untidy or dirty room that suddenly becomes clean and bright can signify the end of moral or spiritual danger; an animal transformed into a human being can represent a re-direction or transcendence of the dreamer's primal instincts; a human transformed into an animal can stand for a descent to the more fundamental levels of the psyche, or for the rediscovery of more natural, spontaneous emotions.

Agents of transformation, such as the wizard, the magician or the shaman, may appear as dream characters. They stand outside the rational, social world, but have the power to change it. Such a figure may be a manfestation of the Trickster archetype (see page 36), who often appears when the ego is in a dangerous situation of its own making, through some kind of misjudgment or moral lapse.

House transformed into a car

The house is the classic symbol of the self. Thus, a house transformed into something else is likely to be a comment by the dream on the state of the dreamer's psyche. A house changing into a car can indicate the importance of movement and progress, but it may also warn of the loss of stable foundations in life. Alternatively, such a dream could be suggesting that the dreamer is losing a sense of his or her own humanity, becoming mechanical, overbearing or ruthless in pursuit of personal or professional objectives.

Words transforming into images

Freud once interpreted an elephant in a client's dream as a pun on the word tromper, *the French word for "to deceive", which sounds like* trompe, *the word for "trunk". Puns of this kind may enable the dreaming mind to give visual form to abstract qualities.*

Myth and Legend

In ancient Greece, *mythos* (from which the English word myth derives) originally meant "word", "saying" or "story", but later its meaning shifted to "fiction" or even "falsehood", as distinct from *logos*, the "word of truth", the currency of historians. However, we now believe that myth contains its own truths, and that many of these truths transcend time and place, resonating with profound meanings at a level deep within the psyche. If dreams and myths stem from the same roots in the collective unconscious, as Jung believed, then it is not surprising that mythical elements may be found in the dreams even of people whose last direct contact with myth is a distant schoolday memory.

Jung recommended the use of myths as a repertoire of parallels which would help a dreamer tease out the meaning of a dream – the process of amplification (see

Mermaid

Combining the symbolism of fish and femininity, the mermaid is a powerful image of the mysterious otherness that haunts and fascinates the male psyche. In dreams, the mermaid typically embodies the Anima – a bringer of secret wisdom and at the same time a seductive temptress, luring the overt, active, male energies of the conscious mind into the uncharted depths of the unconscious.

The hero and the maiden

A common symbol in myth and fairytale is the hero who rescues a young woman. Usually a prince or brave warrior, the hero may represent the noble, unsullied side of the unconscious mind – the part which is not bound by conventional wisdom and dares to set out in search of truth. The maiden herself has often been imprisoned in a castle by her wicked father (or stepfather), her incarceration representing the repression of unconscious wisdom by the inflexible conscious mind.

page 31). With Level 3 dreams, amplification is made easier by the fact that the dream material often contains explicit mythological themes: these represent the archetypal energies of the collective unconscious in personalized form, and indicate the relationship of such energies to the particular life-circumstances of the dreamer.

Mythic images occurring in the dreams of Westerners often call to mind Greek, Egyptian and Christian equivalents – the mythologies with which we in the West tend to be most familiar. The Resurrected God, the Hero, the Saviour, the Trickster, the Wise Old Man and the Young Girl are all recurring archetypes. Sometimes the mythic content is undisguised: a princess in a tower, for example, would be unmistakably a character of legend (its appearance perhaps influenced by a memory of childhood fairytales). However, more oblique references are also encountered, such as a Hero expressed as a star from sport or the movies, or more obliquely still as someone coming valiantly to the rescue in a modern context (perhaps by coming to repair a broken-down car).

The Hero represents virtue, integrity, strength and courage, and redresses the wrongs of the world. This is one of the most powerful of all the archetypes. In a woman's dream it represents the Animus (the assertive male aspect that dwells within the female), while in a man's dream it often serves as a wish-fulfilment – a fantastic extension of the dreamer's ego ideal.

The Hero stands in direct contrast to the Shadow, although part of the task of the dream is to help the dreamer reconcile these two aspects of the self, and thus arrive in due course at more mature and realistic levels of self-understanding.

Dionysos

The Greek god Dionysos, known as Bacchus in Roman myth, was the deity of nature, wine, fertility and divine ecstasy. His followers, a wild roaming band of women known as the Maenads or Baccants, danced in ecstatic frenzy, tearing wild animals apart and eating their raw flesh. In dreams, Dionysos can stand for heightened states of consciousness or a recognition of our deeply instinctive primal energies. Pan, half man and half goat, serves a similar function to Dionysos. A symbol of the instinctive energies, in dreams he reminds us of the beauty of nature, and of the forces of male fertility and growth.

Stars and Planets

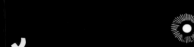
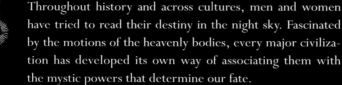

Throughout history and across cultures, men and women have tried to read their destiny in the night sky. Fascinated by the motions of the heavenly bodies, every major civilization has developed its own way of associating them with the mystic powers that determine our fate.

Level 3 dreams about the heavens often convey a sense of the eternal, unchanging nature of ultimate reality. We may feel ourselves to be at one with the stars, our identity absorbed into the far reaches of the universe

Rarely, even in Level 1 and Level 2 dreams, do the stars and planets carry negative connotations, although some dreamers interpret them as emphasizing the insignificance of human life in the face of the vast impersonal forces of the universe.

Occasionally, the dreaming mind will use planets to convey metaphorical meaning, drawing upon their links with mythology. Mars is associated with war, passion and rage, Venus with love and eroticism, Jupiter with fullness, pleasure and well-being, Saturn with wisdom, masculinity and (sometimes) Pan or the Devil.

Planets normally appear singly in dreams, but if there is more than one, it may be their juxtaposition that is important. The sun and moon together may represent the relationship between the conscious and unconscious, rational and irrational, while Saturn and Venus can stand for the relationship between male and female.

Dreams are riddled with paradoxes, and to look out is also to look within. Thus, gazing into the night sky can be a symbol for examining the unconscious, where the infinite possibilities of the imagination make the everyday concerns of the conscious mind seem small and insignificant.

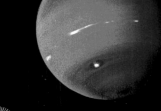

Stars
As well as representing fate and the celestial powers, the stars can stand for the dreamer's higher states of consciousness. A single star shining more brightly than the rest can signify success in competition with others, but may also serve to remind the dreamer of his or her responsibilities to those of lesser ability. The brightest star could also be the one that is closest to destruction.

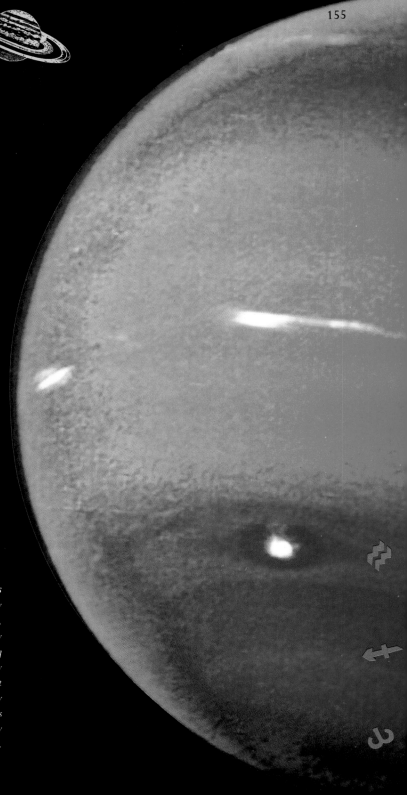

The moon

The moon often represents the feminine aspect, the queen of the night, and the mystery of hidden, secret things. It is also associated with water (because the tides are governed by the moon), and with the imagination. A full moon may indicate serenity and stillness, signifying the dreamer's potential for contemplation. A new moon is an obvious symbol of fresh beginnings.

The sun

The sun has strong connotations of the masculine, the world of overt things, the conscious mind, the intellect, and the father. In dreams, a hot burning sun can indicate the intellect's power to make a desert out of the dreamer's emotional life. Conversely, the sun hidden by clouds can suggest the emotions overruling rationality.

Comets

Although comets may still portend disaster, the modern dreamer is more likely to associate them with a warning of dazzling but temporary success, followed by rapid descent and eventual destruction. They also represent inspiration, ideas and insights flashing brilliantly from the unconscious.

Working with Dreams

The first stage of working with dreams is the art of remembering them. Many people claim never to recall their dreams, and some deny having dreams at all. However, with practice, and the right technique, it is not unusual to remember five or more dreams each morning.

Start with a positive attitude. Remembering dreams is a habit, and can be cultivated. The best way is to tell yourself during the day that you will remember your dreams, and upon awakening lie still for a while, focusing your conscious mind on whatever ideas or emotions have emerged from your sleep, and allowing them through association to prompt dream recall.

Keeping a dream diary makes it possible to build up a detailed, sustained picture of your dream life. Write down (or sketch) everything you can remember – small details as well as main themes – and make a note of any emotions or associations that emerge from the dream's contents. During the day, think back to the dream of the night before, even if its details have faded, and try to re-live the emotions associated with it. Re-read your notes and be patient: it may take weeks or months before you regularly remember your dreams, but success will come if you persevere. To speed things up, occasionally set an alarm clock for about two hours after you usually fall asleep: you will stand a good chance of awakening immediately after the first, dream-laden period of REM sleep.

Some dream researchers advise subjects to collect at least a hundred dreams before starting analysis, as it may take this length of time before the common themes emerge coherently. It is always worth searching for connections with the events of the day, but remember – the dream has a reason for choosing these events, and may be using them to symbolize deeper material. Note anything significant about these events and any memories that they spark off. Such memories may lead back to long-forgotten experiences to which the dream is trying to draw your attention.

Keeping a Dream Record

A dream sketchbook can often capture the mood of a dream better than a written record. Moreover, making notes immediately after waking requires a mental adjustment that will often interpose itself between the dreamer and the dream, whereas a sketch can often be made without losing touch with the remembered experience. The example on these pages is a dream by a 15-year-old girl: her spoken account is given on this page, with a note on the symbolism; the sketch from her visual notebook is reproduced opposite.

"First I saw a hairy caterpillar eating a leaf, which then gradually changed into the keyboard of one of those old upright typewriters. The keys were moving by themselves and the paper coming out of the machine was all crumpled and had glistening raindrops on it — but there was no rain. The paper then appeared on a table and someone had spilt a cup of coffee over it. The caterpillar turned into a butterfly and flew off. Suddenly, I was in a rain storm trying to bring in the laundry, and the caterpillar was there also, crawling along the washing line."

Rain in dreams is often connected with cleansing and purification, while the caterpillar and butterfly together may be symbols of sexual or creative awakening, or of spiritual enlightenment.

Dream Analysis

The best way to analyze dreams is through the recurring themes that emerge from a dream diary. Whether analysis concentrates on these themes or on powerful individual dreams, a good way to start is to separate the dream material into discrete categories: for example, scenery, objects, characters, events, colours, emotions. One should not strive for detailed accuracy: these categories may well overlap, and the memories themselves may be vague or confused. But try not to ignore apparently unimportant details, because these may be the very aspects that carry the most meaning.

Start by selecting something from whichever of the categories appears most relevant, and subject it to the process of Jungian direct association (see page 31). Write down the object (or whatever) in the centre of a piece of paper, hold it in the mind, and note down all associated images and ideas that come to you. Keep returning to the original stimulus. Try to ensure that each association is specific: if the dream contained a red car, it may be its colour, rather than the fact that it is a car, that is of most symbolic significance. When no more associations come to mind, put the paper aside and go on to the next dream symbol with which you want to deal, and so on, until all the desired categories have been covered.

Jung suggested that direct association becomes easier if the dreamer imagines that he or she is describing each element to someone who has never encountered such a thing before. He also advocated elaborating upon direct associations, linking them to any personal reactions or responses that arise for the dreamer in response to the original dream image.

If few associations arise from a dream's main elements, the dream may be operating at Level 1, carrying little representational or symbolic meaning, and simply serving as a reminder of the significance owed to certain events in the dreamer's life. It may be hinting, for example, that particular emotions may need more acknowledgment, or may be providing clues about the solution to problems that have been worrying the dreamer at a conscious level.

If the dream appears to carry a further level of meaning that remains undetectable by direct association, Freudian free association may be helpful, allowing the mind freely to follow a whole chain of thoughts and images set off by the individual dream element, with one idea emerging spontaneously from another. Jung complained that such free and unspecific associations lead the dreamer too far away from the original dream, but Freud's method can reveal significant repressed memories, urges or emotions that direct association may fail to reach.

If the memories and ideas that emerge from dreams are purely personal associations, the chances are that they emerge from a Level 2 dream, but if they seem to be working as archetypal symbols (see page 34) they are probably operating at Level 3. For these "grand dreams" Jung recommended, as a further way of teasing out their meaning, *amplification* (see page 31), a technique to establish parallels between dream symbols and the archetypal imagery stored in the collective unconscious.

Jung stressed that no dream interpretation should be imposed upon the dreamer: the meaning is uncovered only if it provides the dreamer with a self-insight, whether welcome or unwelcome, that rings true. Interpretations should "act" for the dreamer, setting his or her "life in motion again". To be truly effective, a dream interpretation should be confirmed not only by subsequent dreams, but also by subsequent life-events.

Dream Control

Once interpretation has led us into the scenery of our dreams, and once we have recognized their landscapes as the symbols and archetypes of our unconscious mind, we can often begin directly to influence our dream life by trying by various techniques to carry aspects of our waking consciousness into sleep.

The ability regularly to become more conscious in our dreams is known as lucid dreaming (see page 18), and is often found in people who have a high degree of concentration and awareness in waking life. It is also associated with spiritual and occult powers. Tibetan Buddhism teaches that to gain control in the land of our dreams gives us control in the realms after death, where conscious awareness can free the initiate from the illusory cycle of birth and death.

There are several techniques for establishing awareness in dreams, and thus for experiencing them with the conscious mind. Hindu, Buddhist and Western esoteric orders link these methods with more general exercises, such as meditation and self-observation, designed to develop enhanced psychological and spiritual awareness. For example, some Western occultists advocate building up during prolonged and intensive meditation a clear visualization of oneself sitting opposite the physical body, and then transferring consciousness to this. Later, during sleep, this body can be used as the conscious dream body. It is also suggested that by co-hypnosis (which involves two practitioners simultaneously hypnotizing each other) it is even possible consciously to share and control experiences in the dream world.

Shamans attempt to fix a power object of some kind so firmly in the waking mind that it can even be visualized in sleep, reminding them that they are dreaming. The anthropologist Carlos Castaneda was advised by Don Juan, his Yaqui shaman guide to other worlds, to control his dreams and other altered states of consciousness by visualizing his own hands before sleeping, so that if they appeared in his dreams he would become aware that he was dreaming. Shamans also teach that if we vividly re-create the dream worlds in the imagination while we are consciously remembering our dreams, it becomes progressively easier to re-enter them in a conscious state while dreaming. Falling asleep determined to find a particular object, or hear a particular song, may also help to develop conscious control over dreaming.

The *reflection technique* involves asking oneself as often as possible during the day, "How do I know that I am not dreaming now?", and being as specific as possible with the answers. It then becomes easier to recognize an actual dream for what it is, and so assert control over it. A variation on this is the *intention technique,* in which the dreamer is encouraged constantly to tell himself or herself during the day that particular events in the dream world will be recognized as such by the aware, dreaming mind. If, for example, we frequently dream of horses, or trains, or schools, we should impress upon our waking mind that the appearance of such objects in dreams will alert us to the fact of dreaming.

A similar technique is to imagine ourselves dreaming of certain common objects or actions, like climbing stairs or running across a field, and attempt to visualize them as frequently as possible in waking life. Again, when the chosen image occurs in a dream, we become conscious of dreaming.

Autosuggestion, repeating to oneself again and again on the verge of our sleep that conscious awareness *will* emerge in our dreams, can also help.

Recent research on dream control has experimented with laboratory techniques. By recording eye movements or changes in pulse or in breathing, experimenters can detect the moment when REM dreaming commences. Alerting the dreamer with a mild electric shock from a device strapped to the wrist may induce a conscious understanding that a dream is in progress, thus bringing the dream within the dreamer's control .

A somewhat different approach, used by various Eastern traditions and by Jung in his technique of *active imagination,* is to imagine that one is dreaming while awake. Thus we enter a "virtual" waking dream world: everything is seen as an illusion which has been created by the mind, and can be changed at will. By reminding ourselves constantly that we are exercising this will when carrying out every waking action, we can potentially build a bridge between waking and dream consciousness, thus creating a single level of awareness that extends throughout waking, dreaming and dreamless sleep.

A similar technique of mind control is to develop the habit of asking ourselves when remembering dreams why it is that a particularly unusual dream event did not prompt us into realizing that we were dreaming. This technique trains the mind by reminding it of its past failures to alert us to the fact of dreaming, and encouraging it not to repeat such failures.

Many of the above techniques can be used in conjunction with each other as aids to lucid dreaming, as can more conventional methods such as keeping a dream diary or meditation. However, a key requirement for all techniques is patience; do not be too discouraged if the desired results are some time in coming.

It is also vital not to try too hard. Lucid dreaming is achieved by an act of will, but not by an act of teeth-gritting determination. Like any creative activity, it is most readily achieved by a mind that is concentrated, motivated and persistent, but at the same time light and playful.

Solving Problems

The prescription that we should sleep upon problems is well known. Although the conscious ego is inactive while we sleep, some part of the mind continues working on the problems that beset it during the day, so that when we awake the solutions may be already in place.

Sometimes answers are actually given in dreams. A famous example is that of the German chemist Friedrich Kekulé who claimed that his ground-breaking discovery of the molecular structure of benzene, in 1961, came to him in a dream. Working hard on the problem, he fell asleep and dreamed of molecules dancing before his eyes, forming into patterns, then joining like a snake catching its tail in a dream representation of the so-called "benzene ring".

We can sometimes obtain a demonstration of the problem-solving power of the dreaming mind if we visualize an unsolved anagram or mathematical puzzle while drifting to sleep. Instructing the mind to work on the puzzle, just before sleep descends, can often stimulate a dream solution.

The answer may come literally, unfiltered by symbol. The Russian chemist Dmitri Mendeleev, after many fruitless attempts to tabulate the elements according to their atomic weight, dreamed their respective values and subsequently found all but one to be correct, a discovery that led to the publication of his periodic law in 1869.

When dreams offer symbolic rather than literal solutions, interpretation can be more difficult. The scientist Neils Bohr identified the model of a hydrogen atom in 1913 after a dream in which he stood on the sun and saw the planets attached to its surface by thin filaments as they circled overhead. Numerical solutions, in particular, may be conveyed in symbolic form, perhaps using associations lodged deep in the personal unconscious. For example, the number 3 might be indicated by an old three-legged stool from the dreamer's childhood.

One of the most astonishing of all dream discoveries, involving visitation by a dream ghost, is that of H.V. Hilprecht, Professor of Assyrian at the University of Pennsylvania. In 1893, Hilprecht was trying to decipher inscriptions on drawings of two agate fragments believed to come from finger rings, dating from *c.*1300 BC and excavated from the ruins of a temple at Nippur in modern Iraq. Discouraged by lack of success, Hilprecht retired to bed and dreamed that an ancient Babylonian priest appeared before him to inform him with a wealth of background detail that the fragments were not separate rings at all but part of a cylinder that the priests had cut up to make earrings for a statue. If they were put together, the priest told him, the original inscription could be read with ease. Hilprecht awoke and confirmed the truth of his dream, receiving final proof when he examined the fragments in the museum at Istanbul.

Nightmares
Psychological, as well as intellectual problems, can be solved through dreams. Anxiety dreams, for example, can help us recognize important truths about ourselves. In stark contrast to the modern view of "nightmares" is the original meaning of the word as an evil spirit that visited people in their sleep to seduce and so gain possession of them, body and soul. The "mare", or demon, came to women as an incubus (shown in the 18th-century painting by Henry Fuseli, opposite) and to men as a succubus, leaving the dreamer feeling oppressed and overpowered, as if something heavy was pressing on his or her chest. Recent psychology suggests that "nightmares" are dream symbols of unconscious sexual desires (especially repressed passive and masochistic aspects of sexual instinct).

Bibliography and Picture Credits

BIBLIOGRAPHY

Boss, M. (1977) "I Dreamt Last Night": *A New Approach to the Revelations of Dreaming and its Uses in Psychotherapy*. New York: Gardener.

Campbell, J. (1949) *The Hero with a Thousand Faces*. Princeton NJ: Princeton University Press; and London UK: Paladin (1988).

Castaneda, C. (1974) *Tales of Power*. New York: Simon & Schuster .

Dement, W. (1960) "Effect of sleep deprivation". *Science* 131, 1705-1707.

Faraday, A. (1972) *Dream Power: The Use of Dreams in Everyday Life*. London UK: Pan Books.

Garfield, P. (1976) *Creative Dreaming*. London: Futura.

Garfield P. (1991) *The Healing Power of Dreams*. New York and London UK: Simon & Schuster.

Halifax, J. (19 79) *Shamanic Voices*. New York: E. P. Dutton.

Hall, C. S., and Nordby, V. J. (1972) *The Individual and His Dreams*. New York: New American Library.

Hearne, K. (1990) *The Dream Machine*. Wellingborough UK: Aquarian Press.

Hillman, J. (1989) *The Essential James Hillman*. London UK and New York: Routledge.

Inglis, B. (1988) *The Power of Dreams*. London: Paladin.

Jones, R. M. (1978) *The New Psychology of Dreaming*. Harmondsworth UK and New York: Penguin.

Jung, C. G. (1953) *Two Essays on Analytical Psychology*. Second edition. London UK and New York: Routledge (Routledge paperback edition 1992).

Jung, C. G. (1963) *Memories, Dreams, Reflections*. London UK and New York: Routledge (Fontana paperback edition 1967).

Jung, C. G. (1968) *Analytical Psychology: Its Theory and Practice*. London UK and New York: Routledge (Ark paperback edition 1986).

Jung, C. G. (1972) *Four Archetypes*. London UK and New York: Routledge.

Jung, C. G. (1968) *Psychology and Alchemy*. London UK and New York: Routledge (Routledge paperback edition 1980).

Jung, C. G. (1974) *Dreams*. Princeton, NJ: Princeton University Press.

Jung, C. G. (1983) *Selected Writings*. London: Fontana Books (Harper Collins).

Jung, C. G. (1984) *Dream Analysis*. London UK and New York: Routledge.

Kleitman, N. (1963) *Sleep and Wakefulness*. 2nd edition. Chicago: University of Chicago Press.

Mattoon, M. A. (1978) *Applied Dream Analysis: a Jungian Approach*. New York and London UK: John Wiley & Sons.

Mavromatis, A. (1987) *Hypnogogia: The Unique State of Consciousness Between Wakefulness and Sleep*. London UK and New York: Routledge.

Noone, R., and Holman, D. (1972) *In Search of the Dream People*. New York: Morrow.

Snyder, F. (1963) "The new biology of dreaming". *Arch. Gen. Psychiat*. 8, pp 381-391.

Tholey, P. (1983) "Techniques for inducing and manipulating lucid dreams". *Peceptual and Motor Skills*, 57, pp 79-90.

Ullman, M., and Limmer, C. (eds.) (1987) *The Variety of Dream Experience*. New York: Continuum; and London UK: Crucible (1989).

Ullman, M., and Zimmerman, N. (1987) *Working With Dreams*. London UK: Aquarian Press; and New York: Eleanor Friede Books.

Ullman, M., Krippner, S., and Vaughan, A. (1989) *Dream Telepathy: Experiments in Nocturnal ESP*. 2nd edition. Jefferson NC: McFarland.

Van de Castle, R. (1971) *The Psychology of Dreaming*. Morristown, N.J: General Learning Press.

Whitmont, E. C., and Perera, S. B. (1989) *Dreams, a Portal to the Source*. London UK and New York: Routledge.

Notes on the Text

Dreams and sleep

p14 REM sleep was dicovered by the American physiologists Nathaniel Kleitman and Eugene Aserinsky at the University of Chicago, 1953.

Research in the early 1960s revealing four distinct levels of sleep was led by the American physiologist Frederick Snyder.

As early as the 1930s, the American physiologist Edmund Jacobson, among others, noted that eye movement while sleeping is strongly linked with dreaming.

p15 It was the American dream researcher Richard Jones who discovered that brain activity in REM sleep is as different from that of non-REM sleep as it is from waking.

Research into REM deprivation in the 1960s was led by William Dement, one of Kleitman's collaborators at the University of Chicago, and later taken up by Robert Van de Castle at the University of Virginia.

Lucid dreams

p19 Research into lucid dreaming by the American scientist Jayne Gackenbach (b.1946) showed that lucid dreamers appear to suffer less from depression and neuroses.

Precognition and ESP

p20 Professor Hans Bender, of the University of Freiburg, Germany, collected a large number of verifiable precognitive dream accounts, including some from the actress Christine Mylius.

Many dreams foretelling the sinking of the *Titanic* were collected by Professor Ian Stevenson of the University of Virginia.

p21 Louisa Rhine and her parapsychologist husband J.B. Rhine found many race winning dreams among the 1,000 or more precognitive dreams sent to them between 1930 and 1955.

The most intensive attempt to prove the existence of ESP in dreams was carried out by the dream researchers Alan Vaughan and Jessica Utts at the Maimonides Dream Laboratory in Brooklyn, New York, in the 1970s.

Levels of meaning

p23 The Jungian analyst Mary Mattoon believes that proof for the existence of the collective unconscious can also be found in other areas of psychology, linguistics and anthropology.

The nature of dreaming

p24 Research at Hull University, England, found that claims made by an adult that he never slept seemed to be borne out by laboratory tests. He appeared to suffer from none of the symptoms of irritability or loss of concentration usually associated with sleep deprivation.

It was the British psychologist Christopher Evans who first linked the "garbage" approach to dreaming with the operations of computers.

The Nobel prizewinner and urobiologist Francis Crick, who was the first to unravel the genetic code, likened dreams to potentially "parasitical modes of thought".

p25 The British psychologist Anne Faraday and Ian Oswald from the University of Edinburgh led the 1970s research into dream recall and amnesia.

Researchers at the Cincinnati Medical College, Ohio, found that most subjects offered different versions of their dreams when relating them immediately after waking, on the one hand; and on the other hand, when discussing them later with a psychoanalyst.

Freud on dreams

p26 Ernest Jones (1879-1958) is the most extensive and reliable writer on Freud's theories about dreams. He lectured widely in Europe and America, developing Freud's ideas, and publishing between 1953 and 1957 the masterly three-volume biography of Freud's life for which he is best known.

Change and transition

p60 It was the American psychologists Thomas Holmes and Richard Rahe whose research led to the discovery that individuals are prone to physical illness for up to two years after major changes in life-circumstances.

Solving problems

p164 In his classic *On the Nightmare* (1910), Ernest Jones drew a parallel between the medieval belief in "mares" and Freudian dream theory. He found the incubus to be an apt dream metaphor for medieval men's horror of homosexuality and women's fear of their own sexual urges.

The British psychologist Keith Hearne found that more than a half of the nightmare sufferers that he questioned were afraid to go to sleep; some had as many as three nightmares a week.

Dream Index

The Dream Index, which refers to symbols, images, activities and the like, is intended to facilitate the interpretation of dream content.

Page numbers in **bold** type refer to section headings in the Dream Directory; page numbers in *italic* type refer to individual entries in the Dream Directory.

Subject Index